Augmented Reality in E-Commerce

The Future of Online Shopping How AR is transforming retail and consumer experiences

THOMPSON CARTER

Table of Content

TABLE OF CONTENTS

INTRODUCTION

Augmented Reality in E-Commerce: The Future of Online Shopping

In recent years, technology has dramatically transformed the way we shop, altering not only how we discover and purchase products but also how we interact with brands and experience the act of buying itself. Among the most groundbreaking advancements is **Augmented Reality (AR)**, a technology that overlays digital content onto the real world, enabling consumers to visualize products and experiences in immersive ways. As AR continues to gain traction across industries, it is emerging as a pivotal force in **e-commerce**, offering exciting opportunities to redefine online shopping.

This book, *Augmented Reality in E-Commerce: The Future of Online Shopping*, explores the profound impact of AR on retail and consumer behavior, revealing how businesses are leveraging this technology to create more engaging, personalized, and efficient shopping experiences. By offering a comprehensive, jargons-free guide with real-world examples, we aim to demystify the concepts and strategies surrounding AR and provide valuable insights into how it is revolutionizing the way consumers shop online.

As the global retail market grows increasingly competitive, businesses are striving to stand out by adopting innovative technologies that enhance the customer journey. Consumers, too, are seeking shopping experiences that blend convenience, personalization, and entertainment. In this context, AR plays a crucial role by bridging the gap between physical and digital worlds, giving customers the ability to interact with products in ways that were once unimaginable. From visualizing a sofa in your living room to trying on makeup without stepping foot into a store, AR is changing the game for both shoppers and retailers alike.

This book delves deep into the technological foundations of AR, tracing its development and understanding its convergence with other emerging technologies like **Virtual Reality (VR), Artificial Intelligence (AI)**, and **machine learning**. We will explore how these technologies work together to create hyper-personalized shopping journeys and provide tangible benefits to e-commerce businesses. You will also discover how AR improves operational efficiency within the retail supply chain, from **warehouse management** to **real-time product tracking**, offering insights into the full potential of this powerful technology.

But AR's influence in e-commerce doesn't stop there. This book also examines how AR enhances **consumer decision-making**, reduces **return rates**, and drives **brand loyalty** through interactive and immersive product experiences. By integrating

virtual try-ons, **real-time product visualizations**, and **360-degree product views**, AR is making online shopping feel more like a real-world, hands-on experience—offering consumers a deeper connection with the products they're buying.

However, as promising as AR is, its implementation isn't without challenges. In the chapters ahead, we'll address the **technical barriers**, **privacy concerns**, and **user adoption** hurdles businesses must navigate to successfully integrate AR into their operations. We'll also explore best practices, offering practical strategies and advice for businesses that want to stay ahead of the curve by embracing this transformative technology.

As we move further into the future, AR will continue to evolve, becoming even more integrated into our daily shopping habits and reshaping the retail landscape in ways that we have yet to fully comprehend. In this book, you will learn how businesses can prepare for the future by adopting AR into their e-commerce strategies, creating seamless, immersive, and personalized experiences that resonate with today's tech-savvy consumers.

Whether you're an **entrepreneur**, a **retail executive**, a **technology enthusiast**, or someone curious about the future of shopping, this book will equip you with the knowledge and insights you need to understand and leverage **Augmented Reality** in the fast-paced world of e-commerce.

As you read, you'll discover how AR can unlock new possibilities for businesses and consumers alike, helping you better understand its vast potential and how it can help shape the future of online shopping. Through comprehensive research, practical advice, and real-world examples from leaders in the industry, this book will guide you through every stage of AR adoption, ensuring that you are well-equipped to thrive in the future of retail.

CHAPTER 1

WHAT IS AUGMENTED REALITY?

Defining Augmented Reality (AR) and Its Technological Foundations

Augmented Reality (AR) is a technology that blends digital content—such as images, sounds, and other sensory stimuli—into the real-world environment. Unlike Virtual Reality (VR), which immerses users in a completely virtual space, AR enhances the real world by overlaying digital objects onto it in real time. AR creates an interactive experience where users can see and interact with virtual elements in their physical surroundings.

The core of AR involves three main technological components:

1. **Sensors and Cameras**: These devices capture real-world data, allowing the AR system to understand the physical environment. For instance, cameras on smartphones or AR glasses detect the surrounding environment, including objects, surfaces, and spatial awareness.

2. **Processing Power**: AR systems need significant computational power to process the input data from sensors and cameras and then integrate digital elements.

This processing occurs either on the device itself (e.g., smartphone, AR glasses) or in the cloud.

3. **Projection**: This element projects the digital content back into the user's view, blending it with the real-world environment. This could involve visual projections like 3D objects, sound, or even haptic feedback.

Brief History of AR Technology

The concept of Augmented Reality dates back to the early 1960s, with the first recorded use of AR technology being developed by **Ivan Sutherland** in 1968. His creation, known as **"The Sword of Damocles,"** was a head-mounted display (HMD) that could overlay simple 3D shapes into the user's view of the real world, albeit in a very basic form. This device required a bulky and complex setup, which made it impractical for mainstream use at the time.

The next significant breakthrough in AR occurred in the 1990s, when **Tom Caudell** introduced the term "augmented reality" during his work on a project for Boeing. His system helped assembly line workers at Boeing by displaying graphical instructions over their physical environment, helping them work more efficiently.

As technology evolved, AR became more accessible, especially with the development of smartphones. In the early 2000s,

13

researchers and developers began to create more practical and interactive AR applications, bringing the concept closer to what we see today.

Real-World Examples of Augmented Reality

1. **Pokémon   GO   (2016)**

   One of the most well-known AR applications, **Pokémon GO**, brought AR into the mainstream. This mobile game developed by Niantic uses a smartphone's GPS and camera to allow players to catch virtual Pokémon creatures in the real world. The game was a global phenomenon, demonstrating the potential of AR in gaming and entertainment. Players could see Pokémon appear in real-world locations, viewable through their smartphone screens, and interact with them in real time.

   Impact: Pokémon GO proved that AR could create engaging, location-based experiences for millions of users. It highlighted AR's ability to encourage physical activity, provide social interaction, and build community experiences.

2. **IKEA   Place   (2017)**

   IKEA Place is an AR application that allows customers to visualize IKEA furniture in their homes before making a purchase. Using a smartphone or tablet, users can scan

14

their space and place 3D models of IKEA products into the real environment. This helps customers see how the products will look and fit in their living spaces, improving decision-making.

Impact: IKEA Place demonstrated how AR can bridge the gap between online shopping and in-store experiences. It provides customers with a more informed and confident purchasing decision, thus enhancing the online shopping experience. The app is an excellent example of how AR can improve customer satisfaction and reduce return rates in e-commerce.

Conclusion

In this chapter, we have explored the basics of Augmented Reality (AR)—its definition, technological foundations, and the early history that led to its evolution. We also looked at real-world examples such as **Pokémon GO** and **IKEA Place** that highlight how AR is already being used to enhance user experiences in different sectors. As AR continues to develop, it holds immense potential to transform how we interact with the digital world and bridge the gap between the physical and the virtual.

In the next chapter, we will delve deeper into the evolution of e-commerce and explore how AR is integrating with this rapidly growing sector.

CHAPTER 2

THE EVOLUTION OF E-COMMERCE

A Look Back at How E-Commerce Has Evolved

The history of e-commerce can be traced back to the early 1990s, when the internet became publicly accessible and the potential for online commerce started to become apparent. At its inception, e-commerce was seen as a revolutionary way for businesses to reach customers in a more convenient, scalable, and cost-effective manner. However, it was a far cry from the sophisticated, personalized shopping experiences we have today.

1. **The Early Days of E-Commerce (1990s)**
   The first online transaction is often credited to **Stanford student Phil Brandenberger** in 1994, who bought a Sting CD on the site **NetMarket**. During this time, the primary model of e-commerce was simple, static websites offering basic catalog-based shopping. Customers could view product descriptions and images but lacked features like user reviews, personalization, or real-time inventory updates.

16

Key Milestones:

- o **1995**: **Amazon** and **eBay** were founded. Amazon started as an online bookstore, while eBay pioneered online auctions.
- o **1998**: PayPal was launched, providing a secure online payment system that quickly became a standard for online transactions.

2. **The Dot-Com Bubble and Growth (Late 1990s - Early 2000s)**

During the late 1990s and early 2000s, the internet boom fueled a significant growth spurt in online commerce, despite the eventual bursting of the "dot-com bubble" in 2000. Many early e-commerce platforms were not sustainable, but some, like Amazon and eBay, managed to adapt and thrive in the face of adversity.

By the early 2000s, e-commerce had become an integral part of business, offering products ranging from electronics to clothing, books, and more. The rise of **secure online payment gateways** and **shipping logistics** enabled e-commerce businesses to expand their offerings, resulting in increased consumer confidence in online shopping.

3. **The Mobile Revolution (Late 2000s - 2010s)**

The introduction of smartphones and mobile apps in the

late 2000s significantly impacted e-commerce. Consumers could now shop from anywhere, anytime, using their phones. Major companies quickly adapted to this shift by launching mobile-friendly websites and apps to cater to the growing demand for mobile shopping.

Key Developments:

- o **2007**: The first iPhone was released, enabling a new generation of mobile shopping experiences.
- o **2008-2012**: Mobile e-commerce started taking off, with giants like **Amazon, eBay**, and newer platforms like **Shopify** developing mobile applications optimized for purchasing on the go.
- o **2011**: **Amazon** became the first retailer to surpass $1 billion in sales on mobile, demonstrating the huge potential of mobile commerce.

From Basic Online Shopping to Immersive Experiences

While traditional e-commerce was limited to browsing catalogs and completing transactions, the focus gradually shifted toward creating immersive, interactive, and personalized shopping experiences. This shift in approach is largely driven by the integration of emerging technologies such as augmented reality (AR), artificial intelligence (AI), and machine learning.

1. **Personalization** (2010s)

   Personalization emerged as a key trend in e-commerce, thanks to advancements in data analytics and AI. Online retailers began using customer data to tailor product recommendations, promotional offers, and marketing messages based on individual preferences, browsing history, and purchase patterns.

   Real-World Example: **Amazon** is a leader in this area, using advanced algorithms to recommend products to customers based on their previous searches and purchases. This has helped improve conversion rates and customer satisfaction, making shopping feel more customized.

2. **Interactive Shopping (Late 2010s - 2020s)**

   With the development of AR and VR, shopping has evolved into a more immersive experience. Consumers are no longer just browsing products but interacting with them in real-time in digital environments. AR technology allows customers to visualize products in their homes or on themselves before making a purchase, which is particularly beneficial for sectors like furniture, fashion, and beauty.

   Real-World Example: **IKEA's AR app** (IKEA Place) allows users to place 3D models of furniture in their homes through their smartphones, providing a more realistic preview of how products will look in their actual living space.

3. **Social Commerce (2020s and Beyond)** Social media platforms like **Instagram, Facebook**, and **TikTok** have integrated shopping features, turning social networks into shopping hubs. These platforms allow consumers to discover, review, and purchase products directly through the app, eliminating the need to switch to another website. **Social commerce** is especially appealing to younger consumers who prefer seamless, integrated shopping experiences.

Real-World Example: **Instagram Shopping** allows businesses to tag products in their posts and stories, enabling users to purchase directly from the platform. This feature is paired with user-generated content, influencer marketing, and shoppable posts, making it easier than ever for consumers to shop.

4. **Voice Commerce (2020s)** As smart speakers like **Amazon Alexa** and **Google Assistant** become more common, voice shopping is on the rise. Consumers can now use voice commands to search for products, compare prices, and place orders—

making the shopping experience faster and more convenient.

Real-World Example: **Amazon Echo** and **Google Home** allow users to make purchases by simply speaking commands like, "Alexa, order more toothpaste." This voice-enabled commerce is expected to grow as voice recognition technology improves.

Real-World Examples: Amazon, eBay, Shopify

1. **Amazon: A Legacy of Innovation**
   Amazon started as an online bookstore in 1995 but quickly expanded into one of the largest and most diverse e-commerce platforms in the world. Amazon's growth has been driven by its focus on convenience, vast product selection, and its ability to leverage data and AI for personalization. Amazon Prime, Amazon Web Services (AWS), and its continuous innovation in logistics (e.g., drones, robotics) have transformed the e-commerce landscape.

   Key Milestones:

   o **1995**: Launched as an online bookstore.

- o **2005**: Launched Amazon Prime, offering fast shipping and other benefits.
- o **2012**: Entered the hardware market with the Kindle and later, the Echo.

2. **eBay: From Auctions to Global Marketplace**

   eBay, founded in 1995, started as an online auction platform, allowing users to bid on items ranging from collectibles to electronics. Over time, eBay expanded into a global marketplace for new and used goods, offering a wide range of products. It has continued to grow by integrating features like PayPal (now spun off), enabling secure transactions between buyers and sellers.

   Key Milestones:

   - o **1995**: Launched as an online auction site.
   - o **2002**: Acquired PayPal, which later became a key component in online payment systems.
   - o **2008**: eBay expanded internationally and became a leading e-commerce platform in numerous countries.

3. **Shopify: Empowering Entrepreneurs**

   Shopify, founded in 2006, started as an e-commerce platform to help individuals and small businesses create their own online stores. Shopify has since grown into one of the largest e-commerce solutions in the world, offering a comprehensive suite of tools for businesses to manage their online stores, including inventory management, payment processing, and marketing tools.

Key Milestones:

- o **2006**: Launched with a focus on simplifying e-commerce for small businesses.
- o **2015**: Introduced Shopify Plus, targeting larger enterprises.
- o **2020**: Shopify powered over 1 million businesses globally.

Conclusion

From its humble beginnings in the 1990s, e-commerce has undergone a dramatic transformation, fueled by technological advancements and changing consumer expectations. What started as a basic catalog-based shopping experience has evolved into a highly interactive, personalized, and immersive journey, with innovations like AR, mobile apps, and voice commerce leading the way. As we continue to see, companies like **Amazon, eBay**, and **Shopify** are at the forefront of this evolution, demonstrating how technology and customer-centric approaches can reshape the retail landscape. In the next chapter, we will explore how **Augmented Reality** is integrating with e-commerce to create the next generation of shopping experiences.

CHAPTER 3

HOW AR FITS INTO THE E-COMMERCE LANDSCAPE

Understanding the Convergence of AR and E-Commerce

The integration of Augmented Reality (AR) into e-commerce represents a natural evolution in the way consumers interact with online shopping platforms. Over the years, e-commerce has transformed from a simple catalog-based experience to one that focuses on convenience, personalization, and real-time engagement. AR takes this transformation a step further by adding a layer of interactivity and visualization that allows consumers to virtually experience products in their real-world environment before making a purchase.

The convergence of AR and e-commerce is driven by the need for more immersive, engaging, and informative shopping experiences. The challenges that e-commerce faced in the early days—such as the inability to touch, feel, or physically interact with products—are mitigated by AR technology, which creates an interactive digital experience within the physical world. By overlaying digital content, like product images, 3D models, or videos, on top of real-world environments, AR enables consumers

24

to gain a deeper understanding of a product's size, fit, and functionality.

AR enhances the e-commerce journey in various ways:

1. **Visualizing Products in Real Time**: Customers can see products in their own environment, helping them decide if an item is the right fit for their space or personal style.

2. **Improved Product Exploration**: AR allows consumers to interact with products in ways that weren't possible through traditional online shopping. For example, users can zoom in on the details of a product or rotate a 3D model to inspect it from every angle.

3. **Bridging the Gap Between Physical and Digital Shopping**: By using AR, online shoppers can recreate the tactile shopping experience they would typically get in a brick-and-mortar store, such as trying on clothes or virtually testing products like makeup or furniture.

Overview of AR's Potential to Enhance User Experience

AR's potential to elevate the user experience in e-commerce is vast. From improving product visualization to providing interactive and personalized shopping experiences, AR is redefining what online shopping can look like. Here are some key ways AR enhances the user experience:

1. **Product Visualization and Try-Ons**

   AR allows customers to visualize how products will look or fit in their real-world environment before committing to a purchase. Whether it's trying on clothes virtually, visualizing how a piece of furniture fits in a living room, or even testing how a pair of sunglasses looks on a customer's face, AR provides a sense of assurance that the product meets their expectations.

   For example, AR-powered **virtual try-ons** allow customers to see themselves wearing products without physically trying them on, which saves time and reduces the chances of return due to poor fit or style.

2. **Interactive and Engaging Product Exploration**

   One of the most exciting possibilities of AR in e-commerce is the ability for users to interact with products in ways that go beyond what static images can offer. With AR, users can explore a product in 3D, rotate it to examine every angle, and see it in full detail, providing a more engaging and informative shopping experience. This level of interaction can help customers make more informed decisions, reducing uncertainty and boosting purchase confidence.

3. **Personalized Shopping Experiences**

   As AR technology improves, it can be used to tailor shopping experiences for individual users based on their preferences, browsing history, or even their physical environment. For example, AR apps can recommend products based on a customer's past purchases, or even alter the color of a product to match the user's preferred style.

Additionally, AR can help enhance product discovery, providing a more intuitive and personalized way for users to explore new items they may not have considered otherwise.

4. **Reducing Purchase Anxiety and Returns**
   One of the biggest challenges in online shopping is the inability to physically touch and inspect a product before purchasing. This uncertainty often leads to hesitations in making purchases or high return rates when the product doesn't meet expectations. AR can significantly reduce purchase anxiety by giving customers a better understanding of how a product will fit into their lives or surroundings.

For example, seeing a piece of furniture placed in a customer's actual living room or visualizing a dress on their body helps alleviate doubts about size, color, and style. This ultimately leads to a more confident purchasing decision and fewer returns, which benefits both consumers and retailers.

Real-World Examples: AR Apps Used in Retail

Several well-known brands have successfully integrated AR into their e-commerce platforms, transforming the way customers shop and interact with their products. These examples highlight how AR can be used in retail to enhance the shopping experience.

1. **Sephora Virtual Artist (Beauty)**
   Sephora, a global leader in the beauty industry, uses AR through its **Virtual Artist** app to enable customers to virtually try on makeup products before making a purchase. Using their smartphone cameras, users can see how different makeup shades, such as lipstick or eyeshadow, look on their faces in real-time. The app even allows customers to try on different products from various brands, making it a one-stop shop for virtual beauty trials.

   Impact: The **Sephora Virtual Artist** app provides a convenient way for customers to experiment with makeup looks from the comfort of their homes, significantly improving the online shopping experience for beauty products. This AR feature helps customers make more informed decisions, reducing the chances of purchasing a product that doesn't suit their skin tone or style.

2. **Gucci AR Sneakers (Fashion)**

   Gucci, a high-end fashion brand, has embraced AR in a unique way through its **Gucci AR sneakers** feature. The brand's app allows users to try on sneakers virtually, using AR technology to superimpose digital sneakers onto the user's feet via their smartphone's camera. This feature gives customers the ability to see how different sneaker styles look on their feet, helping them make purchasing decisions without having to visit a physical store.

   Impact: Gucci's integration of AR into their shopping experience allows customers to visualize luxury products, such as sneakers, in a more personal and interactive way. By providing a digital fitting room experience, Gucci enhances customer engagement and drives sales in a competitive retail market.

3. **L'Oreal AR Try-Ons (Beauty)**

   L'Oreal has introduced AR technology to revolutionize the beauty industry with its **AR Try-On** app. Similar to Sephora's Virtual Artist, L'Oreal allows customers to try on makeup virtually. The app features a wide range of products, including foundation, lipstick, eyeshadow, and even hair color. The AR technology uses facial recognition to map the user's face and place the digital makeup on their features in real-time.

Impact: L'Oreal's AR Try-Ons give customers a realistic preview of how beauty products will look on them, eliminating the need for physical testers in stores. This is particularly useful in the era of COVID-19, where health and safety concerns have made traditional makeup testing difficult. The AR experience also boosts confidence in online purchasing and provides a more engaging way to discover new products.

Conclusion

Augmented Reality is poised to revolutionize the e-commerce landscape by transforming the way consumers interact with products online. The convergence of AR and e-commerce not only bridges the gap between the digital and physical worlds but also enhances the user experience through personalized, interactive, and immersive features. As we've seen in the real-world examples of **Sephora**, **Gucci**, and **L'Oreal**, AR has the power to improve product visualization, reduce return rates, and ultimately drive sales. As AR technology continues to evolve, the potential for enhancing the online shopping experience will only expand, paving the way for more engaging and innovative retail experiences. In the next chapter, we will explore how AR is being applied to specific sectors of e-commerce, including fashion, home furnishings, and beauty.

CHAPTER 4

THE TECHNOLOGY BEHIND AR

Overview of the Technologies Enabling AR

Augmented Reality (AR) relies on a combination of hardware and software to create seamless, interactive experiences that blend digital content with the real world. As AR technology has evolved, a variety of devices and systems have been developed to enable users to interact with AR experiences. Here, we will explore the primary hardware components and devices that make AR possible, including smartphones, VR headsets, and AR glasses.

1. **Smartphones and Tablets**

   Smartphones and tablets are the most widely used devices for AR experiences today. These devices are equipped with various sensors, cameras, and processing power that allow AR applications to function efficiently. Smartphones, with their built-in cameras, GPS, accelerometers, and gyroscopes, enable AR apps to detect the user's environment and overlay digital content accordingly.

   o **Key Features**:

- **Camera**: Captures real-time video of the environment.

- **Accelerometer and Gyroscope**: Detects the device's orientation and movement, which helps in accurately placing digital objects in the real world.

- **GPS**: Provides location-based services in AR apps, such as augmented navigation or geo-tagging.

o **Real-World Example**: AR apps like **Pokémon GO** rely heavily on smartphones' built-in sensors to detect the environment and superimpose digital content over the physical world.

2. **Virtual Reality (VR) Headsets**
While primarily associated with immersive virtual environments, some VR headsets can also support augmented reality experiences by blending virtual elements into the real world. These devices typically use a combination of cameras, sensors, and motion tracking to place virtual objects in a user's view of the physical world.

o **Key Features**:

- **Cameras and Sensors**: Track the user's movement and orientation, allowing virtual objects to interact with the real world.

32

- **Display**: Head-mounted displays (HMDs) provide a wide field of view for users to experience augmented content.
  - **Real-World Example**: **Microsoft HoloLens** is one of the most notable AR-capable VR headsets, offering mixed reality experiences that combine virtual and real-world elements.

3. **AR**   **Glasses**

AR glasses are wearable devices that provide an immersive AR experience while allowing users to maintain their awareness of the real world. Unlike VR headsets, AR glasses are designed to overlay digital content directly onto the user's field of view without completely blocking out the physical environment. These devices are typically smaller, lighter, and more comfortable for long-term wear compared to VR headsets.

- **Key Features**:
  - **See-through Display**: Digital content is projected onto transparent lenses so that users can still see the real world.
  - **Sensors and Cameras**: Track the user's surroundings and interact with real-world objects.
  - **Voice and Gesture Controls**: Allow for hands-free interaction with AR content.

33

- o **Real-World Example**: **Google Glass** and **Microsoft HoloLens** are two of the most well-known AR glasses, used in a variety of industries from retail to healthcare.

Basics of AR Development Tools and Platforms

Developing AR applications requires specialized tools and platforms that provide the necessary frameworks to create, design, and deploy AR experiences. These platforms simplify the process of integrating AR technology into applications, making it accessible to developers without requiring deep expertise in computer vision or 3D modeling.

1. **ARKit** **(Apple)**

   ARKit is Apple's framework for building AR applications on iOS devices. Introduced in 2017, ARKit enables developers to create AR experiences that use the device's camera, motion sensors, and processing power to place digital content in the real world. ARKit supports features like object detection, environment mapping, and face tracking, allowing for highly interactive and immersive AR applications.

   - o **Key Features**:

- **Scene Understanding**: ARKit can detect horizontal and vertical surfaces (e.g., floors, tables) to place virtual objects accurately.
- **Face Tracking**: Using the front-facing camera, ARKit can track a user's facial expressions and overlay filters or animations on their face.
- **Motion Capture**: ARKit can detect the user's movement and orientation, allowing for interactive AR experiences.

o **Real-World Example**: ARKit is used in apps like **IKEA Place** (virtual furniture placement) and **L'Oreal Makeup Genius** (virtual makeup try-ons).

2. **ARCore**   **(Google)**

ARCore is Google's counterpart to Apple's ARKit and is designed for Android devices. ARCore enables developers to build AR apps that use the camera and sensors to detect and track the environment, enabling virtual objects to interact with real-world surroundings. ARCore supports both basic AR features, such as surface detection and object placement, as well as more advanced features like augmented images and motion tracking.

o **Key Features**:

- **Environmental Understanding**: ARCore detects surfaces and ambient light to help place virtual objects realistically in the user's environment.
- **Augmented Images**: ARCore can recognize and track specific images, allowing for interactive experiences.
- **Cloud Anchors**: This feature allows multiple users to share AR experiences in the same physical space.

  o **Real-World Example**: ARCore powers AR experiences in apps like **Google Lens** (object recognition) and **Nike's AR Try-On** feature (virtual sneaker fitting).

3. **Unity**

   Unity is one of the most widely used game engines and is also a popular platform for developing AR applications. With its powerful 3D engine and extensive support for AR development, Unity allows developers to create high-quality AR experiences that work across multiple devices, including smartphones, tablets, and AR glasses.

   o **Key Features**:

   - **Cross-Platform Development**: Unity supports both ARKit and ARCore, enabling developers to build AR apps for both iOS and Android devices.

- **Real-time Rendering**: Unity's real-time 3D rendering capabilities enable the creation of high-fidelity AR environments and objects.
- **Asset Store**: Unity's Asset Store provides a wide range of pre-built AR models, environments, and tools that developers can use to accelerate development.

o **Real-World Example**: Unity powers AR apps across industries, including **Walmart's AR shopping app** and **BMW's AR car configurator**.

4. **Vuforia**

Vuforia is another popular AR development platform, designed for creating AR applications across mobile devices and wearables. It supports both marker-based and markerless AR experiences, offering features like image recognition, object tracking, and spatial awareness.

o **Key Features**:

- **Image Recognition**: Vuforia can detect and track images, enabling interactive experiences based on specific visuals.
- **Object Recognition**: It also supports tracking of 3D objects in the real world.

- **Cloud Recognition**: Vuforia's cloud database can store image and object data for scalable AR experiences.

o **Real-World Example**: Vuforia is used in applications like **Mattel's AR-enabled toys** and **L'Oreal's AR makeup try-ons**.

Real-World Examples: ARKit, ARCore, Unity

1. **ARKit**

As mentioned earlier, ARKit is used in various iOS apps to create immersive AR experiences. Some notable examples include:

o **IKEA Place**: An app that lets users visualize furniture in their homes using ARKit. This is a great example of how ARKit's environment mapping capabilities allow customers to see how products will fit and look in their real-world space.

o **L'Oreal Makeup Genius**: This app allows users to try on makeup virtually using ARKit's face tracking technology, offering a personalized experience based on the user's facial features.

2. **ARCore**

Google's ARCore powers several popular AR apps on Android, including:

- **Google Lens**: An app that uses ARCore to recognize objects and provide real-time information about them, such as identifying landmarks or translating text in images.

- **Nike's AR Try-On**: This feature lets customers virtually try on sneakers using ARCore's environmental and motion tracking technology, making it easier for them to visualize how shoes will look and fit.

3. **Unity**

Unity is widely used for AR game development and creating high-fidelity AR experiences. A few examples include:

- **Walmart's AR Shopping App**: Powered by Unity, this app allows users to interact with products in-store and learn more about them through AR experiences.

- **BMW's AR Car Configurator**: Unity is used to build an AR app where users can customize and visualize vehicles in real-time in their environment, helping them make informed decisions before purchasing.

Conclusion

The technology behind AR is driven by a combination of hardware and software innovations that have evolved over time. With devices such as smartphones, AR glasses, and VR headsets, AR is becoming increasingly accessible and immersive. Tools like **ARKit**, **ARCore**, **Unity**, and **Vuforia** provide developers with the frameworks needed to create rich, interactive AR experiences. These platforms enable the creation of personalized, engaging, and highly functional AR applications that are transforming industries, including e-commerce. As the technology continues to improve, the potential for AR to revolutionize the way we shop, interact with products, and engage with the world around us is immense.

CHAPTER 5

ENHANCING PRODUCT VISUALIZATION

How AR Helps Customers Visualize Products in Their Own Space

One of the most significant challenges in traditional online shopping is that customers cannot physically interact with products before making a purchase. This can lead to uncertainty and hesitation, particularly when it comes to items like furniture, home decor, and fashion accessories, where size, fit, and style are crucial factors in the decision-making process. Augmented Reality (AR) addresses this challenge by allowing customers to visualize products in their real-world environment before committing to a purchase.

AR technology enables a virtual representation of a product to be superimposed onto the user's surroundings in real-time, providing an interactive and immersive experience. The key benefit of AR in product visualization is that it allows consumers to see how a product will look in their space, on their body, or in their everyday life, without needing to physically interact with it. This ability to "try before you buy" has a profound impact on customer confidence, helping them make informed decisions that align with their preferences and needs.

Some of the specific ways AR enhances product visualization include:

1. **Spatial Awareness**: AR allows customers to see products in context, such as visualizing how a piece of furniture will fit into their living room or how a new pair of glasses will look on their face. The ability to view a product at different angles, sizes, and distances gives a more accurate representation than a static image.

2. **Product Customization**: With AR, users can also experiment with different variations of a product, such as color, size, or style, and see how those changes affect the overall look. This interactive customization helps customers make choices based on their personal preferences and space constraints.

3. **Improved Decision-Making**: Seeing a product in one's own environment helps eliminate doubts about its fit, size, and aesthetics. This feature is particularly useful for items like furniture, home decor, fashion accessories, and cosmetics, where physical attributes like size and color are essential in making purchase decisions.

4. **Reduction in Returns**: By providing a more accurate and detailed visualization of a product in the customer's own space or on their body, AR reduces the likelihood of a

mismatch between customer expectations and the actual product. This ultimately leads to fewer returns and exchanges, which is a significant benefit for both retailers and consumers.

Real-World Examples: Warby Parker, Home Depot

Several leading brands are leveraging AR to enhance the customer shopping experience, making it easier for consumers to visualize products and make more confident purchase decisions. Let's take a closer look at how **Warby Parker** and **Home Depot** have successfully integrated AR into their e-commerce platforms.

1. Warby Parker: Virtual Try-On for Eyewear

Warby Parker, a popular eyewear brand, has revolutionized the way consumers shop for glasses by incorporating AR technology into its mobile app. The **Warby Parker Virtual Try-On** feature allows users to see how different frames look on their face using the front-facing camera of their smartphone.

How it Works:

- Users can choose from a wide variety of frames in the app and virtually "try them on" by using their phone's camera to see how the glasses will look on their face.

43

- The app overlays the selected frames in real-time onto the user's face, accurately adjusting the fit and positioning to match the person's facial features.

Impact:

- **Personalized Experience**: Warby Parker's AR feature makes the process of choosing glasses much more personalized, as it allows customers to experiment with different styles and sizes in real-time.
- **Convenience**: Customers can now shop for glasses from the comfort of their own home without needing to visit a store, helping to bridge the gap between in-store and online shopping.
- **Reduction in Returns**: By giving customers a better idea of how frames will look on their face before they buy, AR helps reduce the number of returns due to poor fit or style preferences.

This innovation in eyewear retail has been so successful that it has helped increase customer engagement, improve the shopping experience, and drive sales growth for Warby Parker.

2. **Home Depot: Visualizing Furniture and Home Improvement Products**

Home Depot, a leader in the home improvement sector, has adopted AR technology to help customers visualize how products like furniture, appliances, and home decor items will look in their homes. The company introduced the **Home Depot Project Color App** and other AR tools that allow consumers to view products in their own environment using their smartphones or tablets.

How it Works:

- Customers can use the app to scan their space and see how products, such as furniture, paint colors, and appliances, would look in their home.
- The app can place virtual items in a room in real time, allowing customers to see the size, scale, and appearance of the product within the context of their existing décor.
- Home Depot's AR tools also allow customers to experiment with different combinations of products, such as seeing how various paint colors look against a specific wall.

Impact:

- **Improved Product Fit**: AR helps customers make better-informed decisions about size and style by showing them how the product fits into their space before purchasing.
- **Increased Sales**: By providing an interactive and engaging way to shop for home improvement items, Home Depot encourages customers to visualize their

projects before purchasing materials and products, leading to higher conversion rates.

- **Convenience and Time Savings**: Customers no longer need to visit physical stores to get a sense of how products will look in their homes. They can visualize everything from the comfort of their homes, making the shopping process more convenient.

By using AR to help customers make more informed decisions about their purchases, Home Depot has significantly improved its customer experience, helping customers feel more confident in their choices.

Conclusion

Enhancing product visualization is one of the most powerful applications of Augmented Reality (AR) in e-commerce. By allowing customers to see products in their own space, on their body, or in a personalized context, AR provides a level of interaction and immersion that was previously unavailable through traditional online shopping methods. The ability to visualize a product in real-time, customize it, and see how it fits into one's environment can help reduce the uncertainty that often comes with online shopping.

Brands like **Warby Parker** and **Home Depot** are leading the way in using AR to transform the shopping experience, demonstrating the immense potential of AR to enhance product visualization and improve decision-making. As AR technology continues to evolve, we can expect even more innovative ways for retailers to provide immersive and personalized shopping experiences that help customers make more informed and confident purchasing decisions.

CHAPTER 6

IMPROVING CONSUMER DECISION-MAKING

How AR Influences Purchase Decisions by Providing Interactive and Immersive Experiences

One of the most significant ways that Augmented Reality (AR) is transforming the e-commerce landscape is by directly influencing consumer decision-making. The decision to make a purchase is often driven by emotions and perceptions, which can be shaped by the shopping experience itself. Traditional online shopping presents challenges, such as the inability to touch, feel, or try out a product, leading to uncertainty and hesitation. AR helps bridge this gap by offering interactive and immersive experiences that allow consumers to engage with products in a much more meaningful way.

AR creates an experience that goes beyond static images and descriptions, enabling consumers to interact with products in real-time and visualize how they will look or fit in their actual environment. By providing this level of interaction, AR encourages customers to make more confident and informed decisions. Here's how AR enhances the consumer decision-making process:

1. **Real-Time Interaction**: AR allows users to actively engage with products in a dynamic way. For example, a customer can rotate a 3D object, zoom in on product details, or try on virtual clothing, which mimics the experience of interacting with physical products in-store. This interactivity is far more engaging than simply viewing a product from a single static image or reading a description.

2. **Visualizing Fit and Aesthetics**: With AR, customers can see how a product will look in their own space, on their body, or in relation to their environment. For instance, they can visualize how a piece of furniture will fit in their living room or how a pair of shoes will look on their feet. This visual confirmation removes a significant amount of uncertainty, making it easier for consumers to make decisions about size, fit, color, and style.

3. **Instant Feedback**: AR provides immediate feedback on the customer's choices. For example, when selecting a product variant, such as a different color or size, AR can show how those changes affect the look or functionality of the product. This feedback helps consumers feel more in control of their decision-making process, reducing hesitation and encouraging faster purchases.

4. **Reducing Cognitive Load**: Traditional online shopping often involves the mental strain of comparing multiple products and visualizing how they would fit in one's life. AR simplifies this process by allowing consumers to see different options in a single, interactive view. This not only saves time but also alleviates the cognitive load that comes with imagining how a product will fit into their world.

5. **Building Confidence**: By allowing customers to test products virtually, AR gives them a sense of certainty about their choices. They can experiment with different combinations, check for fit or style, and be more confident that the product will meet their expectations. This confidence directly impacts the likelihood of a purchase.

Real-World Examples: L'Oreal's AR Try-On, Nike's AR Fitting Rooms

Several leading brands have already adopted AR technology to enhance the shopping experience and influence consumer decision-making. These brands have created interactive, immersive AR tools that help customers make more informed decisions, whether they're purchasing beauty products, apparel, or accessories. Here are two notable examples of AR's role in improving consumer decision-making:

1. L'Oreal's AR Try-On (Beauty)

L'Oreal, one of the world's largest beauty brands, has integrated AR technology into its online shopping experience with its **AR Try-On** feature. Through this app, customers can virtually try on makeup products, such as lipstick, eyeshadow, foundation, and mascara, using their smartphone's front-facing camera.

How it Works:

- Customers can use the app to see how different makeup products look on their face in real-time.
- The app overlays digital makeup on the user's face, allowing them to view the look from various angles.
- L'Oreal's AR Try-On uses advanced facial recognition to map the user's facial features and apply makeup products in a realistic and natural way.

Impact on Decision-Making:

- **Visualizing Fit**: Customers can see how different shades and products suit their skin tone, which reduces uncertainty and helps them make more confident decisions about their purchases.
- **Enhanced Confidence**: Virtual try-ons eliminate the risk of purchasing a product that doesn't match the customer's preferences, reducing the likelihood of returns and encouraging repeat business.

51

- **Personalization**: By allowing users to experiment with different looks, L'Oreal's AR Try-On feature helps personalize the shopping experience, making it feel more tailored to the individual customer's needs.

L'Oreal's AR Try-On feature provides a fun, interactive way to experiment with beauty products, driving consumer engagement and improving the likelihood of successful purchases.

2. Nike's AR Fitting Rooms (Fashion & Footwear)

Nike has also incorporated AR into its e-commerce strategy with its **AR Fitting Room** feature, which allows customers to virtually try on shoes using their smartphones. With this tool, Nike enhances the online shopping experience by giving customers a better sense of how shoes will fit and look before they buy.

How it Works:

- Using the camera on their smartphones, customers can point their devices at their feet to see how different shoe styles fit on their feet.
- The AR fitting room allows customers to view the shoes in different colors and designs, all in real-time as they move around and shift their feet.
- This feature can be used both in-store and online, allowing customers to visualize how shoes look while

shopping from the comfort of their own homes or in Nike stores.

Impact on Decision-Making:

- **Instant Visualization**: Nike's AR Fitting Room gives customers immediate, accurate visualization of how shoes will look on their feet, helping to reduce doubts about size, fit, and style.
- **Increased Engagement**: The interactive nature of the AR feature encourages customers to engage more with the brand, exploring different styles and combinations in a playful and immersive manner.
- **Reduced Returns**: By allowing customers to virtually try on shoes and see how they look, the likelihood of purchasing shoes that don't fit or meet their expectations is reduced, leading to fewer returns.

Nike's AR Fitting Room exemplifies how AR can create an engaging, fun, and interactive experience that influences purchase decisions by giving customers the tools to visualize how products fit and look on their bodies.

Conclusion

Augmented Reality (AR) plays a pivotal role in enhancing consumer decision-making by providing interactive, immersive experiences that allow customers to visualize products in real time. By overcoming the limitations of traditional online shopping, AR helps customers feel more confident in their purchase decisions, whether they're buying makeup, shoes, or furniture. AR features like **L'Oreal's AR Try-On** and **Nike's AR Fitting Room** showcase the power of AR to improve the shopping experience, reduce uncertainty, and ultimately drive sales. As AR technology continues to evolve, we can expect even more brands to leverage it to create personalized, engaging, and confident shopping experiences that meet the needs and preferences of today's consumers.

CHAPTER 7

PERSONALIZING THE SHOPPING EXPERIENCE

How AR Can Be Used for Hyper-Personalized Shopping Experiences

In today's competitive retail environment, offering a personalized shopping experience is crucial to attracting and retaining customers. Personalization goes beyond just addressing the consumer by name; it involves tailoring every aspect of the shopping experience to the individual's preferences, needs, and behaviors. Augmented Reality (AR) has emerged as a powerful tool for enhancing personalization, creating hyper-personalized experiences that engage customers in new, interactive ways.

AR enables a level of personalization that traditional online shopping experiences can't provide. By combining real-time interaction with digital content and leveraging user data, AR creates a shopping experience that is unique to each customer. Here's how AR is used to provide personalized shopping experiences:

55

1. **Customizing Product Visualizations**: AR allows customers to view and interact with products in real-time, and this can be personalized based on individual preferences. For instance, AR tools can adjust the appearance of a product—such as its color, size, or features—based on what the user selects or likes. This dynamic customization of products provides a highly personalized experience that aligns with the user's tastes.

   o **Example**: A customer shopping for furniture can use an AR app to visualize a chair in their living room, but they may also be able to adjust the chair's color or material to suit their existing decor. This customization increases the likelihood of the customer making a purchase because they see exactly what the item will look like in their own space.

2. **Personalized Recommendations**: AR can enhance product recommendations by offering personalized suggestions based on user preferences and previous behavior. By tracking how users interact with virtual objects or products through AR, retailers can provide tailored recommendations that suit their individual styles or needs.

   o **Example**: If a user spends more time viewing a particular style of furniture or clothing using AR, the app could recommend similar products based on that interest. This dynamic recommendation engine not only creates a more personalized shopping experience but also helps guide the customer through the purchasing decision.

3. **Location-Based Personalization**: AR tools can also leverage location data to provide personalized shopping experiences. For example, AR apps can detect where the customer is located and show them products or offers available nearby or specific to their geographic area. This could be especially helpful in physical stores, where customers can access AR experiences to learn about promotions, new arrivals, or special offers based on their current location.

   o **Example**: A customer walking through a retail store could use an AR app that guides them to items on sale or informs them about products that match their shopping history, making their in-store shopping experience more personalized and efficient.

4. **Facial Recognition and Customization**: Advanced AR applications can integrate facial recognition to offer hyper-personalized experiences in certain sectors like beauty, fashion, and eyewear. By analyzing a customer's face, AR can suggest products that complement their facial features or skin tone, offering a

tailored experience that helps users make decisions with more confidence.

- o **Example**: AR-powered apps for makeup brands can recommend the best foundation shades or lipstick colors based on a user's complexion. Similarly, eyewear brands can suggest frames that suit a customer's face shape.

5. **Augmenting Personal Style**: AR can be used to enhance a customer's personal style by suggesting new looks, outfits, or accessories that match their existing wardrobe. By virtually trying on different styles, customers can experiment with combinations they might not have considered otherwise.

- o **Example**: A customer could use an AR-powered fashion app to try on various clothing styles and see how they would look together before deciding to make a purchase. The app could even suggest new items to add to the mix based on their selections.

Real-World Examples: Amazon's AR Tools, AI Integration in AR

Leading brands are already using AR to offer personalized shopping experiences that go far beyond the traditional online shopping model. Here's how **Amazon** and the integration of **AI in AR** are making strides in personalization:

1. Amazon's AR Tools

Amazon has long been at the forefront of e-commerce innovation, and its AR tools play a critical role in personalizing the shopping experience. The company's **AR View** feature in the **Amazon app** allows customers to visualize products in their own homes before making a purchase. This tool enables users to see how everything from furniture to home decor will look in their living spaces, providing a more personalized shopping experience.

How it Works:

- **AR View** lets customers view 3D models of products and place them within their homes using their phone's camera. Customers can adjust the product's size and orientation, ensuring it fits perfectly within their space.
- The app allows customers to rotate and scale products to match their preferences and see how they blend with existing furniture or decor.

Impact on Personalization:

- **Increased Confidence**: By visualizing products in their homes, customers are able to make better-informed decisions, leading to fewer returns and higher satisfaction.

59

- **Personalized Space Planning**: Customers are able to experiment with how products will fit into their homes, making the experience more tailored to their needs.
- **Real-Time Customization**: AR tools allow customers to virtually "try on" products in their own environment, offering a level of customization and interactivity that traditional product images cannot match.

2. AI Integration in AR

Artificial Intelligence (AI) plays an important role in enhancing AR by enabling deeper personalization. Through AI, AR systems can analyze user behavior, preferences, and interactions with products to offer customized suggestions and recommendations in real time.

How AI Works with AR:

- **Behavioral Insights**: AI can track how users interact with AR elements, such as which products they spend the most time viewing, and use that information to make recommendations.
- **Learning User Preferences**: AI-powered AR systems can adapt to user preferences over time. For example, by analyzing which colors, styles, or types of products a user gravitates toward, the system can present more tailored suggestions.

- **Facial Recognition and Customization**: AI can help enhance AR experiences by analyzing facial features, body shape, or other personal characteristics to offer highly personalized recommendations. For instance, an AR app for fashion could suggest outfits that complement a user's body type.

Real-World Example:

- **L'Oreal's AI-Powered AR**: L'Oreal's **AR makeup app** combines AR and AI to offer personalized makeup recommendations based on a user's unique facial features. The app scans the user's face and suggests the best shades for foundation, lipstick, and eyeshadow. This AI-driven personalization helps users find products that work best for their complexion and style, creating a more tailored and satisfying shopping experience.

Impact on Personalization:

- **Tailored Shopping Journeys**: AI integration with AR enables e-commerce platforms to offer personalized product recommendations and experiences based on individual preferences, behavior, and data.
- **Enhanced User Engagement**: By providing users with more relevant, customized experiences, AI-powered AR

tools enhance engagement and increase the likelihood of purchase.

Conclusion

Personalizing the shopping experience is a key factor in today's competitive e-commerce market, and AR is an essential tool in creating hyper-personalized experiences. By enabling customers to interact with products in real-time, visualize them in their environment, and receive personalized recommendations, AR helps make shopping more engaging, efficient, and satisfying.

Real-world examples like **Amazon's AR tools** and the **AI integration in AR**, as seen with **L'Oreal's** app, demonstrate how brands can create tailored shopping journeys that meet the unique preferences and needs of each consumer. As AR and AI technologies continue to evolve, we can expect even more sophisticated and individualized shopping experiences that enhance customer satisfaction and drive sales. By providing a personalized, immersive, and interactive environment, AR is transforming e-commerce into a truly customer-centric experience.

CHAPTER 8

INCREASING CUSTOMER ENGAGEMENT

The Role of AR in Keeping Customers Engaged and Increasing Brand Loyalty

In a world where consumers are constantly bombarded with information and options, keeping customers engaged is more challenging than ever. One of the most effective ways to increase customer engagement and build brand loyalty is by offering immersive, interactive experiences that resonate with consumers. Augmented Reality (AR) plays a critical role in this process, providing brands with the tools to captivate and engage customers in meaningful ways.

AR goes beyond traditional marketing tactics by blending the digital and physical worlds, creating experiences that are not only visually captivating but also interactive. By providing a unique, immersive experience, AR encourages customers to spend more time with a brand, boosting engagement and fostering a deeper emotional connection. Here's how AR can help brands engage customers and increase loyalty:

1. **Interactive**   **Experiences**:

   AR allows customers to engage with a brand in a way that feels personal and fun. The interactivity of AR experiences invites users to explore products or brand content in a hands-on manner, which is much more engaging than passive forms of advertising.

   o **Example**: Instead of simply browsing through product images, customers can virtually try on items, explore 3D models, or interact with products in real-time. This interactive engagement is both enjoyable and informative, which increases the time customers spend on a brand's platform.

2. **Gamification**:

   AR offers brands an opportunity to introduce gamified elements to their marketing strategies. By incorporating game-like features, such as challenges, rewards, or interactive missions, AR can turn the shopping or brand experience into a fun and immersive activity.

   o **Example**: Brands can create AR scavenger hunts, quizzes, or contests that encourage customers to interact with their products, explore virtual environments, and unlock rewards, creating a sense of excitement and motivation to return.

3. **Enhanced**   **Brand**   **Experience**:

   AR has the power to provide unique, memorable

64

experiences that increase emotional connection with a brand. By offering innovative ways to engage with products and services, brands can stand out from competitors and establish themselves as forward-thinking and customer-centric.

- o **Example**: Through AR, customers can experience a brand's values and personality in ways that resonate emotionally. Whether through storytelling, virtual brand ambassadors, or interactive product demos, AR fosters a deeper connection to the brand.

4. **Personalization**:

AR allows for highly personalized experiences by tailoring content based on customer preferences, previous interactions, and behaviors. This personalized approach increases relevance and engagement, as customers feel that the brand understands their needs and desires.

- o **Example**: AR can display personalized product recommendations, allow customers to try products on virtually, or even enable them to customize products in real time, providing a unique experience every time they interact with the brand.

5. **Building Brand Loyalty Through AR**: AR not only attracts customers but can also be used to reward them for their engagement. By offering exclusive

AR experiences or rewards for continued interaction with the brand, companies can encourage repeat visits and long-term loyalty.

- o **Example**: AR can create a sense of exclusivity by offering AR-based loyalty programs where customers can unlock special features, discounts, or content after completing certain actions or interacting with the brand over time.

Real-World Examples: IKEA's Augmented Catalogs, Coca-Cola's AR Campaigns

Several leading brands have already harnessed the power of AR to engage customers and strengthen brand loyalty. Let's take a closer look at two examples of how **IKEA** and **Coca-Cola** have integrated AR into their strategies to increase engagement:

1. **IKEA's Augmented Catalogs**

IKEA, the Swedish furniture and home goods giant, has become a leader in using AR to engage customers and make their shopping experience more interactive. IKEA's **IKEA Place** app allows customers to visualize how furniture and home decor items will look in their own homes before making a purchase. This tool is a perfect example of how AR can be used to increase engagement by creating an immersive, interactive experience.

How it Works:

- Customers use their smartphones to scan their environment and see how specific pieces of furniture will fit in their space.
- The app uses AR to place accurate 3D models of IKEA products into the user's real-world environment, helping customers determine size, style, and overall fit.

Impact on Engagement and Loyalty:

- **Immersive Experience**: By allowing customers to interact with IKEA's products in their own homes, the app provides a more engaging, personalized shopping experience than traditional catalogs or online shopping methods.
- **Increased Confidence**: The AR feature helps customers make more confident decisions, reducing the likelihood of returns and fostering loyalty to the IKEA brand.
- **Convenience**: The app allows customers to visualize products without leaving their homes, making it easier and more convenient for them to make purchases.
- **Repeat Visits**: The app also encourages customers to return and explore different furniture combinations, creating a continuous, engaging experience that builds long-term brand loyalty.

2. Coca-Cola's AR Campaigns

Coca-Cola has used AR technology in several marketing campaigns to increase consumer engagement and build emotional connections with its brand. One of the most notable examples is Coca-Cola's **AR-enabled cans**, which featured interactive content when scanned through a mobile device.

How it Works:

- Coca-Cola launched a special series of cans that had AR codes printed on them. When customers scanned these codes using their smartphones, they were able to unlock exclusive, interactive content, including games, videos, and personalized messages.
- In some cases, the AR experience involved virtual animations, such as a character dancing or performing a fun action on the screen as the user scanned the can, creating a playful and memorable interaction.

Impact on Engagement and Loyalty:

- **Interactive Fun**: Coca-Cola's AR campaigns turned ordinary cans into interactive experiences, offering consumers an engaging and fun way to connect with the brand.
- **Brand Awareness**: By incorporating AR into their products, Coca-Cola created buzz and drew attention to

their limited-edition cans, helping to reinforce brand recognition and loyalty.

- **Emotional Connection**: The playful nature of the AR experience fostered a positive emotional connection with the brand, as customers were excited to interact with the product in a new and innovative way.

- **Encouraging Repeat Purchases**: The use of AR encouraged customers to collect cans to see different interactive content, which helped drive repeat purchases and created excitement around Coca-Cola products.

Conclusion

AR is playing a pivotal role in increasing customer engagement by offering immersive, interactive experiences that captivate and hold the attention of consumers. By providing personalized and fun interactions with products, brands can create lasting emotional connections that foster loyalty and repeat business. **IKEA's augmented catalogs** and **Coca-Cola's AR campaigns** are just two examples of how AR is being used creatively to enhance brand engagement. As AR technology continues to evolve, it will become an increasingly important tool for brands to differentiate themselves in the marketplace, create memorable experiences, and build long-term customer loyalty.

CHAPTER 9

REDUCING RETURN RATES

How AR Can Help Reduce Product Returns by Improving Purchase Confidence

One of the most significant challenges in e-commerce is managing product returns. Returns are costly for businesses, both in terms of shipping and restocking, and they often lead to customer dissatisfaction. In fact, a major reason for returns is customer dissatisfaction with the product's fit, color, size, or overall appearance. Augmented Reality (AR) is emerging as a powerful tool to help reduce return rates by improving purchase confidence, allowing customers to make more informed decisions before completing their transactions.

AR technology addresses key issues that lead to returns by allowing customers to interact with products virtually, giving them a more realistic sense of how products will meet their needs. Here's how AR helps improve purchase confidence and ultimately reduces return rates:

1. **Visualizing Fit and Style:**
   One of the most common reasons for returns in the apparel industry, for example, is poor fit or the product

70

not looking as expected once it arrives. AR allows customers to visualize how products will look on their body or in their space before making a purchase. By enabling virtual try-ons or product simulations, AR helps eliminate uncertainty about size, color, and fit.

- o **Example**: A customer shopping for a jacket can use an AR tool to see how the jacket will look on their body, adjusting the size and style to match their preferences. This experience gives them a clear understanding of how the jacket will fit in real life.

2. **Reducing Uncertainty About Product Details**: Online shopping often leaves customers with questions about the appearance of a product—will the color look the same as in the picture? Is the material as expected? AR allows customers to inspect products in greater detail, including examining textures, colors, and size in 3D, thus reducing uncertainty and encouraging more confident purchasing decisions.

- o **Example**: With AR, a customer can examine the intricate details of a pair of shoes or a piece of furniture, rotating the product to view it from all angles, which gives them a better understanding of the product's quality and features.

3. **Interactive Product Exploration**: AR can enhance the exploration of a product by providing

interactive experiences where customers can virtually try on clothes, see how furniture fits into their home, or visualize how makeup will look on their face. The more involved and interactive the experience, the more confident a customer becomes in their decision.

- o **Example**: In the beauty industry, AR tools let customers see how different makeup products will look on their skin tone, giving them a more accurate representation of the product's effects before they purchase.

4. **Personalized Recommendations Based on AR Interactions**:

   AR can also provide personalized experiences, such as offering product recommendations based on the customer's previous interactions with the product, or on their preferences as identified through AR tools. This tailored approach can help customers find exactly what they are looking for, reducing the chances of returns due to dissatisfaction.

   - o **Example**: A customer using an AR tool to try on multiple clothing items can be recommended other styles, sizes, or colors that better suit their preferences, leading to a more satisfying purchase.

Real-World Examples: Apparel Brands Using AR to Simulate Try-Ons

Several leading apparel brands have integrated AR technology into their online shopping experiences to simulate try-ons, significantly improving purchase confidence and helping reduce return rates. Here's a closer look at how some brands are successfully using AR to simulate product try-ons:

1. **Zara: Virtual Fitting Rooms**

Zara, one of the world's leading fashion retailers, has implemented AR technology in several of its stores and online platforms to simulate fitting rooms and improve the online shopping experience. Zara's **AR feature** allows customers to visualize how clothing items would look on their body without trying them on physically.

How it Works:

- Zara's AR tool allows customers to point their smartphones at a designated area in stores or scan QR codes to activate virtual models wearing the latest outfits.
- Online, customers can upload images of themselves or use AR to superimpose the clothing items on their body, giving them an idea of how the clothes will look, fit, and move in real life.

73

Impact on Reducing Return Rates:

- **Increased Confidence**: By offering virtual try-ons, Zara helps customers visualize how clothes will fit and look in real life, reducing hesitation and uncertainty.
- **Personalized Fit**: AR allows users to adjust sizes and styles to see how they affect the overall look, giving customers a more tailored experience.
- **Fewer Returns**: With a better understanding of how the clothing will look and fit, customers are more likely to be satisfied with their purchase and less likely to return the items.

2. **Gap: AR Try-On for Footwear**

Gap, another major apparel retailer, has leveraged AR to improve its footwear shopping experience. The brand introduced an AR feature to allow customers to virtually try on shoes and see how they fit their feet before making a purchase.

How it Works:

- The AR feature enables customers to scan their feet with their smartphone cameras and visualize how shoes will look on them, adjusting the size, color, and style as desired.

- The AR tool also allows customers to check for proper fit by visualizing how shoes look from different angles, including side and top views.

Impact on Reducing Return Rates:

- **Improved Fit Accuracy**: By allowing customers to virtually try on shoes and check their fit, Gap helps reduce common issues related to poor fit, which is a leading cause of footwear returns.
- **Better Product Choice**: The AR tool enables customers to experiment with different colors and styles, ensuring they make a more informed decision.
- **Fewer Returns**: By helping customers make more confident decisions about size and style, Gap has seen a reduction in returns, particularly related to footwear.

3. **ASOS: Virtual Try-On for Clothing**

ASOS, a global fashion retailer, has integrated AR and AI to allow customers to virtually try on clothing and accessories using their smartphones or computers. ASOS's **AR try-on feature** combines with the brand's extensive product catalog to give customers a more accurate representation of how the clothing will look on them.

How it Works:

- The AR feature uses a model's body type and measurements to simulate how the clothes will look on the user. It offers a more accurate representation of fit by allowing users to input their measurements or upload a photo of themselves.
- The AR tool uses 3D rendering and machine learning to display clothing accurately on the user's image.

Impact on Reducing Return Rates:

- **Better Fit and Style Understanding**: Customers can get a clear sense of how clothes will look and fit before purchasing, reducing the uncertainty that often leads to returns.
- **More Personalized Shopping**: By allowing users to visualize clothing on their own bodies, ASOS personalizes the shopping experience and helps customers make decisions that are more suited to their personal style and fit preferences.
- **Fewer Returns**: With a more accurate visual representation of the product, customers are more likely to purchase the right size and style, leading to fewer returns due to fit or dissatisfaction.

Conclusion

AR is a powerful tool for reducing return rates by enhancing purchase confidence. By offering immersive and interactive experiences, AR allows customers to visualize products in a realistic context before making a decision, thereby reducing uncertainty about fit, color, size, and overall style. Apparel brands like **Zara**, **Gap**, and **ASOS** are already seeing the benefits of AR in improving their customers' shopping experiences and reducing the number of returns. As AR technology continues to evolve, its ability to help customers make more informed and confident purchase decisions will only grow, leading to a more streamlined and satisfying e-commerce experience for both retailers and consumers.

CHAPTER 10

VIRTUAL TRY-ONS

Deep Dive into Virtual Fitting Rooms for Fashion and Accessories

Virtual try-ons have become one of the most transformative applications of Augmented Reality (AR) in e-commerce, especially in the fashion and accessories sectors. Traditional online shopping, while convenient, has often fallen short in helping consumers evaluate fit, size, and appearance, leading to uncertainty and, frequently, returns. Virtual fitting rooms, powered by AR, solve this problem by allowing customers to virtually try on clothing, accessories, and even makeup from the comfort of their own homes.

The concept of virtual try-ons uses AR technology to create digital simulations of products, enabling customers to see how these items will look on them in real time. Unlike static images or videos, virtual fitting rooms allow for interactive, dynamic, and highly personalized experiences. They give customers the ability to adjust sizes, colors, and even see the products from different angles, which improves their confidence in making a purchase.

Key features of virtual try-ons in fashion and accessories include:

1. **Realistic Product Visualization**:
Virtual fitting rooms allow customers to see how products will look on their body or face with accurate details, such as size, fit, and color. This helps eliminate the uncertainty about how an item will appear in real life, which is particularly important for clothing and accessories.

   o **Example**: A shopper can see how a dress fits their body shape, or a customer can try on sunglasses to see if the frames suit their face shape.

2. **Personalization**:
Virtual try-ons can be tailored to an individual's unique features, such as body measurements, face shape, or skin tone. By integrating AI and machine learning, these platforms can offer personalized product suggestions based on the user's preferences and past interactions.

   o **Example**: The system may recommend clothing styles that complement a user's body type or suggest glasses frames that match the shape of their face.

3. **Interactivity**:
Virtual fitting rooms are interactive, allowing customers to rotate, zoom in, and adjust the product in real-time. This provides a more engaging and informative experience than simply browsing static images.

   o **Example**: A customer can rotate a pair of shoes 360 degrees to inspect them from all angles or can adjust the length of a jacket in the virtual try-on experience.

4. **Convenience**:

   One of the main benefits of virtual try-ons is the ability to try on products without leaving home. This is especially useful for customers who are shopping online but want the tactile experience of trying on clothes or accessories before making a purchase.

   o **Example**: Instead of going to a store to try on several outfits, a customer can quickly try on multiple pieces of clothing virtually, making shopping faster and more efficient.

5. **Reducing   Return   Rates**:

   Virtual try-ons help reduce return rates by improving purchase confidence. When customers can see how an item will look on them before buying, they are more likely to be satisfied with their purchase, which results in fewer returns.

   o **Example**: A customer who virtually tries on a pair of jeans and sees that they fit perfectly is less likely to return them than someone who buys the jeans without a clear idea of how they will fit.

Real-World Examples: ASOS Virtual Try-On, Ray-Ban Stories

Several fashion and accessories brands have adopted AR technology to create virtual try-on experiences, enhancing the shopping process and providing customers with a more interactive and personalized way to shop. Here are two notable examples of how brands like **ASOS** and **Ray-Ban** have integrated virtual try-ons into their e-commerce strategies.

1. **ASOS Virtual Try-On (Fashion)**

ASOS, a major online fashion retailer, has implemented AR technology in its online shopping experience through its **Virtual Try-On** feature, designed to help customers visualize how clothing will look and fit on their bodies. This tool combines AR with a detailed virtual model of the user, allowing them to virtually "try on" clothing items.

How it Works:

- **Body Scanning and Measurement**: ASOS's virtual try-on tool uses a combination of body scanning and AI to model clothing on a virtual version of the customer. Users can input their body measurements to get a more accurate simulation of how the clothing will look.
- **Real-Time Visualization**: Customers can see how different clothing items will look on their virtual avatar, adjusting the fit and trying on multiple outfits. The

technology also allows users to interact with the 3D model, rotating it to view clothing from different angles.

Impact:

- **Personalized Fit**: The virtual fitting room provides customers with a more personalized shopping experience by simulating how clothes will look based on their body shape and size.
- **Enhanced Shopping Experience**: With real-time adjustments and the ability to try on multiple outfits, ASOS enhances the overall shopping experience, encouraging customers to spend more time exploring the product range.
- **Reduced Returns**: By helping customers visualize how clothing fits before purchasing, ASOS is able to reduce the number of returns due to incorrect sizes or poor fit, which is a common problem in fashion e-commerce.

2. **Ray-Ban Stories (Eyewear)**

Ray-Ban, in partnership with **Facebook**, has launched an AR-powered virtual try-on feature for its eyewear products through its **Ray-Ban Stories** platform. This feature allows customers to virtually try on a wide range of eyeglasses and sunglasses to see how the frames will look on their face in real time.

How it Works:

- **Facial Recognition Technology**: Ray-Ban Stories uses AR and facial recognition to superimpose eyewear products onto the customer's face via their smartphone camera or the Ray-Ban app. The virtual try-on experience is highly accurate, providing a realistic view of how the frames will fit and look.

- **Variety and Customization**: Customers can choose from various styles, colors, and shapes, and see how each frame looks on their face. The technology adjusts the size and orientation of the frames to ensure they appear naturally on the user's face.

Impact:

- **Enhanced Decision-Making**: Ray-Ban's virtual try-on tool helps customers make more informed decisions by giving them a clear sense of how different eyewear styles will look on their face.

- **Improved Customer Engagement**: The AR-powered try-on feature creates an engaging, interactive shopping experience that encourages users to explore different eyewear options and experiment with various styles.

- **Reduced Return Rates**: By allowing customers to try on frames virtually, Ray-Ban helps minimize the risk of returns due to poor fit or dissatisfaction with the product.

Conclusion

Virtual try-ons are transforming the fashion and accessories industries by providing customers with a highly interactive and personalized shopping experience. AR technology allows shoppers to see how products will look on them in real-time, improving their confidence in their purchase decisions. Whether it's trying on clothing, eyewear, or other accessories, virtual fitting rooms eliminate much of the uncertainty that leads to returns, making the online shopping experience more satisfying for both customers and retailers.

Real-world examples like **ASOS's Virtual Try-On** and **Ray-Ban Stories** show how AR can be effectively used to create more engaging and personalized shopping experiences. As AR technology continues to evolve, we can expect even more innovative applications in the fashion and accessories industries, further enhancing the way customers shop online and reducing the likelihood of returns.

CHAPTER 11

AR IN HOME FURNISHING AND DECOR

How AR Helps Customers Visualize Furniture and Home Products in Their Spaces

Shopping for home furnishings and decor can be a particularly challenging task when done online. Unlike clothing or electronics, many home products like furniture, rugs, or artwork require careful consideration of how they will fit and look within the specific layout and design of a customer's home. To address this challenge, Augmented Reality (AR) has emerged as a game-changer, allowing customers to visualize home products in their own spaces before making a purchase.

AR helps eliminate much of the uncertainty that traditionally comes with online shopping for home goods by enabling users to digitally place 3D models of products in their homes via their smartphones, tablets, or AR glasses. This immersive technology gives customers a realistic preview of how items will look in their rooms, ensuring that they meet expectations in terms of size, style, and color.

Here's how AR enhances the home shopping experience:

1. **Space and Fit Visualization**: AR allows customers to see how furniture or decor will fit into the layout of their room, ensuring that the size of the product is suitable for the available space. This helps to avoid common issues like purchasing an item that's too large or too small for the intended space.

    o **Example**: A customer shopping for a couch can see how the piece fits into their living room, adjusting its position and scale in real time to make sure it complements the existing furniture and layout.

2. **Style and Aesthetic Visualization**: Besides size and fit, AR also helps customers assess how a product's style, color, and texture will match the overall aesthetic of their home. By virtually placing furniture, rugs, or decor items into a room, users can quickly determine whether the product complements their existing decor or if it clashes with other elements in the room.

    o **Example**: A customer can try different color variations of a lamp or switch between multiple styles of coffee tables to see which one looks best in their living room.

3. **Realistic Product Rendering**: AR provides highly detailed 3D models of home products

that simulate their appearance in real-world lighting conditions. These products can be viewed from multiple angles and distances, giving customers a better understanding of how the items will look when they are physically present in their home.

- o **Example**: AR tools can show how a rug will look on a specific floor type (wood, tile, etc.) and in different lighting conditions, giving users a true-to-life preview of the item.

4. **Interactive   Experience**:

Unlike static images or videos, AR offers a more engaging and interactive experience, enabling users to move products around and adjust them in their space. This level of interaction enhances the decision-making process by making the experience feel more like a hands-on trial.

- o **Example**: A customer can use an AR tool to virtually arrange and rearrange different pieces of furniture, testing various configurations and layouts before making a purchase.

5. **Customization**:

AR allows customers to customize products in real time, such as changing the color, material, or size of a piece of furniture. This feature gives shoppers the flexibility to create exactly what they want without having to rely solely on the pre-set options available in a catalog.

    o   **Example**: A customer shopping for a sofa could adjust the upholstery fabric or choose between different leg styles, instantly visualizing the changes in their room.

Real-World Examples: IKEA Place, Houzz

Several companies in the home furnishings and decor industry have successfully incorporated AR into their e-commerce platforms, providing customers with the tools they need to visualize products in their homes and make more confident purchasing decisions. Here are two prime examples of AR in home decor:

1. **IKEA Place**

IKEA, the Swedish furniture giant, has been a leader in utilizing AR to help customers visualize how products will look in their homes. **IKEA Place** is a mobile app that allows customers to use AR technology to place true-to-scale 3D models of IKEA furniture into their homes using a smartphone or tablet.

How it Works:

- **AR Visualization**: IKEA Place uses the device's camera and AR technology to scan the customer's environment and place 3D models of furniture in real-time. This allows users to see how different pieces of furniture, such as sofas, chairs, tables, and shelving, fit into their spaces.

- **Real-Time Adjustments**: Customers can move the virtual furniture around the room, adjust its scale, and view it from multiple angles to ensure it fits both physically and aesthetically within the room.

Impact on Customer Experience:

- **Accurate Fit and Placement**: By helping customers see exactly how a product will look and fit in their homes, IKEA reduces uncertainty and the likelihood of returns due to size or style mismatches.
- **Enhanced Shopping Experience**: The AR feature provides a more interactive and personalized shopping experience, encouraging customers to explore different configurations and product choices in their own space.
- **Reduced Returns**: IKEA's AR tool leads to fewer returns, as customers are more confident in their purchase decisions after seeing how the furniture will look in their homes before buying.

2. **Houzz: AR for Home Design**

Houzz, an online platform for home remodeling and design, has also embraced AR technology to help customers visualize home products in their living spaces. The **Houzz app** offers an AR tool called **View in My Room 3D**, which allows customers to see how furniture, decor, and other home improvement items will look in their space.

How it Works:

- **View in My Room 3D**: Customers can use this AR tool to place a virtual product, such as a piece of furniture or a light fixture, into their home environment. The app uses the device's camera to scan the room and provide a life-like simulation of how the product will look in real time.
- **Room Customization**: Houzz allows users to experiment with various colors, materials, and configurations of furniture and home decor, helping them find the perfect match for their interior design.

Impact on Customer Experience:

- **Increased Purchase Confidence**: By allowing customers to virtually place products in their homes, Houzz helps them make more informed and confident decisions, reducing the chances of buying items that don't fit or match their existing decor.
- **Personalized Shopping**: The AR tool enhances the overall shopping experience by enabling customers to see

products tailored to their unique living spaces, making it feel more personal and relevant.

- **Convenience**: The app offers a convenient, at-home solution for visualizing and shopping for home decor, saving time and effort compared to in-store shopping or relying solely on photos.

Conclusion

AR is revolutionizing the home furnishings and decor industry by allowing customers to visualize how products will look in their homes before making a purchase. This immersive technology provides a highly interactive and personalized shopping experience, helping customers make more confident decisions about product fit, style, and color. By using AR tools like **IKEA Place** and **Houzz's View in My Room 3D**, brands are enhancing the customer experience, reducing returns, and increasing overall satisfaction. As AR technology continues to evolve, we can expect even more innovative ways for customers to engage with home products, making the online shopping experience more convenient, enjoyable, and reliable.

CHAPTER 12

AR FOR AUTOMOTIVE RETAIL

Virtual Vehicle Showrooms and How AR Enhances Car-Buying Experiences

The automotive industry has always been at the forefront of integrating technology into the retail experience, and Augmented Reality (AR) is no exception. Car-buying has traditionally been an in-person, showroom-based experience, where customers inspect vehicles, interact with salespeople, and take test drives. However, with the advent of AR, the automotive retail process is evolving into a more interactive, immersive, and personalized journey that transcends the physical limitations of traditional dealerships.

AR enhances the car-buying experience by offering virtual vehicle showrooms, allowing customers to visualize, configure, and interact with cars in an entirely new way. With AR, potential buyers can explore car models in 3D, customize vehicle features, and even experience the vehicle in different environments—all without stepping foot in a dealership.

Here are some ways that AR is enhancing the automotive buying experience:

1. **Virtual Vehicle Showrooms**: AR technology allows consumers to browse and explore different vehicle models virtually. By simply using their smartphones or tablets, buyers can view 3D models of cars, zoom in on specific features, and interact with the vehicle as if it were physically in front of them.

   o **Example**: A customer could point their smartphone at a space in their garage and view a full-sized, virtual car in the space, rotating the vehicle to examine it from different angles.

2. **Interactive Vehicle Configurators**: AR tools can be integrated into vehicle configurators, enabling customers to personalize their vehicles in real time. Consumers can select different colors, trim levels, wheel designs, and even interior options, all while visualizing their customizations in 3D. This gives buyers the ability to see how their ideal car would look before making a decision.

   o **Example**: A potential buyer can virtually "build" a car with their preferred features and view how the vehicle changes with each customization, helping them make more informed choices about what they want.

3. **Enhancing the Test-Drive Experience**: Traditional test drives allow customers to experience how a car performs on the road, but AR can take this

93

experience to a new level by simulating different driving environments. For instance, AR can be used to project information about a car's features or driving capabilities as customers interact with the vehicle.

- o **Example**: In a virtual showroom, customers could simulate how a car performs in various driving conditions, like city streets, highways, or even off-road environments, all from the comfort of their home.

4. **Personalized Marketing and Sales**: AR allows car dealerships to create personalized sales experiences for customers. Based on the customer's preferences, AR can suggest car models, colors, and features that are most likely to resonate with them, making the shopping experience more relevant and engaging.

- o **Example**: A customer who has shown interest in electric vehicles (EVs) might be presented with a virtual showroom featuring only electric cars, with the option to further customize the vehicle's features.

5. **Virtual Test Drives**: Through AR, customers can take virtual test drives in various environments, enabling them to assess a vehicle's features, performance, and appearance without physically driving the car. This not only saves time but also helps

customers experience the vehicle in scenarios that may be difficult to simulate in person.

- o **Example**: AR-powered virtual test drives allow customers to experience the car's handling, acceleration, and technology features through an immersive simulation.

Real-World Examples: Audi's AR Car Configurator

Audi, the German luxury car manufacturer, has been a leader in integrating AR into its car-buying experience. Audi's **AR car configurator** is a perfect example of how AR technology can be used to enhance the car-buying process and provide a more immersive and personalized experience for customers.

1. **Audi's AR Car Configurator**

Audi's **AR car configurator** allows customers to virtually design and customize their vehicles using AR technology. Instead of relying on static images or videos, customers can interact with a 3D model of the car and customize various aspects of the vehicle in real-time.

How it Works:

- **Virtual Customization**: Using the AR configurator, customers can change the color, trim, wheels, and other features of the car. As they make adjustments, the AR model updates in real-time, allowing them to see how the changes affect the overall appearance of the vehicle.

- **Immersive 3D Viewing**: The AR configurator enables customers to place the car in their environment, such as on their driveway, to get a better sense of its size and how it fits into their surroundings.

- **Interactive Experience**: Customers can rotate the car, zoom in to examine details, and even explore the interior of the car, all through their smartphone or tablet.

Impact on Customer Experience:

- **Personalized Vehicle Selection**: The AR configurator allows customers to visualize their customizations in a highly interactive and personalized way, which makes the car-buying process more enjoyable and informative.

- **Convenience**: Audi's AR tool eliminates the need for customers to visit a physical dealership to see and configure their vehicle. They can perform the entire process from the comfort of their home, which is especially convenient in the age of online shopping.

- **Improved Decision-Making**: By offering a detailed, real-time visualization of the car and its features, the AR configurator helps customers make more informed decisions and reduces the uncertainty that often accompanies major purchases like cars.

2. **BMW's AR Experience: AR for Vehicle Presentation**

BMW has also embraced AR technology to enhance the automotive retail experience. **BMW's AR feature** allows customers to explore vehicles and their features through their smartphones, bringing cars to life in the customer's real-world environment.

How it Works:

- **3D Models**: Customers can view highly detailed, full-scale 3D models of BMW cars through their smartphone's AR functionality, allowing them to inspect the exterior and interior features of the vehicle.
- **Vehicle Customization**: The AR tool allows users to interact with the car's features, such as wheels, colors, and trims, and visualize these changes in real-time.

Impact on Customer Experience:

- **Enhanced Engagement**: BMW's AR experience offers a more engaging and interactive way for customers to explore the cars, which helps foster a deeper connection to the brand.

- **Improved Visualization**: By viewing the car in their environment, customers can make more confident decisions regarding size, color, and style.

Conclusion

AR is revolutionizing the car-buying process by providing immersive and interactive experiences that help customers make more confident purchasing decisions. Virtual vehicle showrooms and AR-powered configurators allow customers to visualize cars in 3D, customize them in real-time, and even experience them in different environments. As demonstrated by **Audi's AR car configurator** and **BMW's AR experience**, AR enhances the customer experience by making the car-buying journey more personalized, convenient, and engaging. As AR technology continues to evolve, we can expect even more innovations in the automotive retail space, transforming the way customers shop for cars and ultimately increasing sales and customer satisfaction.

CHAPTER 13

AR IN COSMETICS AND BEAUTY

How AR is Revolutionizing Beauty Product Trials and Virtual Makeovers

The beauty and cosmetics industry has long been rooted in the tactile experience of trying on products in-store. Whether it's testing foundation shades, experimenting with lipstick colors, or trying out new eyeshadows, in-store experiences have allowed consumers to physically interact with products to determine what works for them. However, Augmented Reality (AR) is transforming this experience by enabling virtual beauty product trials and makeovers.

AR is revolutionizing the beauty shopping experience by offering virtual try-ons that allow consumers to experiment with a wide range of makeup products without the need for physical samples. By using a smartphone, tablet, or computer camera, AR tools can overlay makeup onto a user's face in real-time, offering a highly interactive and personalized experience.

Here's how AR is reshaping beauty product trials:

1. **Virtual Product Trials**: AR enables customers to digitally try on makeup products such as foundation, lipstick, eyeshadow, mascara, and more. These virtual try-ons offer a highly realistic simulation of how products will look on the user's skin, ensuring they find the right colors and shades before making a purchase.

   o **Example**: Customers can see how a specific lipstick shade looks on their lips or experiment with different foundation shades to find the perfect match.

2. **Real-Time Visualization**: Unlike traditional makeup sampling, which can be messy or require multiple visits to a store, AR allows customers to instantly see how products will look on their face in different lighting conditions. This real-time interaction eliminates guesswork and helps consumers make confident purchasing decisions.

   o **Example**: A customer trying on different makeup products through an AR app can rotate their face, adjusting the angles to see how the makeup appears from various perspectives.

3. **Customizable Makeovers**: AR-powered virtual makeover tools allow users to try different makeup looks, experiment with bold and unique styles, or follow professional tutorials. Consumers can see

how specific products work together and get inspiration for new looks, all without the need for physical products.

    o   **Example**: AR tools can help users create customized eye makeup looks by experimenting with different eyeshadow, eyeliner, and mascara combinations.

4. **Personalized**   **Recommendations**: AR systems can integrate AI to provide personalized product recommendations based on a user's skin tone, facial features, and preferences. By analyzing the user's face, the AR system can suggest makeup products that complement their natural features.

    o   **Example**: AR apps can analyze a person's complexion and suggest foundation shades that match their skin tone, or recommend lipsticks that suit their individual style.

5. **Hygiene**   **and**   **Safety**: In light of the COVID-19 pandemic, AR technology has also become a safer alternative to in-person product testing. Customers no longer have to physically apply makeup in-store or use communal testers, reducing the risk of contamination and promoting hygiene.

    o   **Example**: Virtual try-on tools offer a hygienic and convenient solution to testing makeup products, allowing consumers to experiment without the need for shared physical testers.

Real-World Examples: Sephora Virtual Artist, L'Oreal AR Try-On

Leading beauty brands have successfully adopted AR technology to enhance the beauty shopping experience, providing customers with virtual product trials, personalized makeovers, and a more convenient way to explore new beauty products. Let's take a closer look at **Sephora's Virtual Artist** and **L'Oreal's AR Try-On** to understand how these tools are revolutionizing the cosmetics industry:

1. **Sephora Virtual Artist (Beauty)**

Sephora, one of the largest global beauty retailers, has pioneered the use of AR in cosmetics with its **Virtual Artist** tool. This AR-powered feature allows customers to try on makeup virtually and explore different looks from the comfort of their own homes.

How it Works:

- **AR Try-On**: Sephora Virtual Artist uses the camera on a smartphone or tablet to overlay makeup products onto the user's face in real-time. Customers can see how different shades of lipstick, eyeshadow, and blush look on their face without physically applying the products.

- **Live Customization**: Users can adjust the shades, change the intensity, and experiment with different makeup combinations, allowing them to create a completely personalized look.
- **Product Recommendations**: Based on a customer's past preferences and the products they interact with, the app provides personalized product recommendations, making it easier for customers to find the products that work best for them.

Impact on Customer Experience:

- **Enhanced Engagement**: Sephora Virtual Artist offers an engaging and interactive experience that encourages customers to explore different products and try new looks.
- **Convenience**: Customers no longer need to visit a physical store to test products. They can use the tool at home, experimenting with various makeup items and combinations.
- **Increased Confidence**: By allowing customers to see how makeup products look on their skin tone before purchasing, Sephora reduces the uncertainty that often leads to returns, resulting in higher customer satisfaction and loyalty.

2. **L'Oreal AR Try-On (Beauty)**

103

L'Oreal, a global leader in the beauty industry, has implemented AR technology in several of its brands, providing virtual try-on solutions for makeup, hair color, and skincare products. The **L'Oreal AR Try-On** tool allows customers to experience makeup products digitally and visualize how they will look on their face in real-time.

How it Works:

- **AR Makeup Try-On**: Using a smartphone or tablet camera, users can apply virtual makeup products to their face, seeing how various foundation, lipstick, eyeshadow, and mascara products will look before making a purchase.
- **Color and Style Customization**: L'Oreal's AR tools also allow users to try out different hair colors, giving them a visual preview of how they would look with a new hair color before committing to a permanent change.
- **Realistic Virtual Applications**: L'Oreal's AR technology uses advanced facial recognition and AI to simulate makeup and hair color applications, providing users with highly accurate and lifelike previews.

Impact on Customer Experience:

- **Increased Purchase Confidence**: L'Oreal's AR Try-On tool helps customers make informed decisions about the

104

products they purchase, reducing the likelihood of returns due to dissatisfaction with the product's color or texture.

- **Hygienic and Convenient**: AR Try-On offers a safe, hygienic way to test makeup products without the need for physical samples or testers, making it an attractive solution in the post-pandemic world.

- **Personalized Shopping**: By analyzing users' facial features, L'Oreal's AR tools provide customized recommendations that enhance the shopping experience and make it easier for customers to find products suited to their individual needs.

Conclusion

AR technology is transforming the beauty and cosmetics industry by providing customers with interactive, personalized, and immersive ways to trial products. With tools like **Sephora Virtual Artist** and **L'Oreal AR Try-On**, consumers can experiment with makeup and skincare products virtually, try on different looks, and receive personalized recommendations—all from the comfort of their homes. This not only enhances the shopping experience but also boosts customer confidence, leading to better purchase decisions and reduced returns. As AR technology continues to evolve, we can expect even more innovative beauty experiences that will reshape how customers engage with brands and products in the future.

CHAPTER 14

AR IN GROCERY AND FOOD SHOPPING

Virtual Food Experiences and How AR Improves the Grocery Shopping Journey

Grocery shopping is one of the most routine tasks in consumers' lives, but it is also one that is ripe for innovation. Traditional grocery shopping involves physical visits to a store, where customers browse aisles, pick up products, and make their selections. However, with the rise of e-commerce and mobile technology, the grocery shopping journey is shifting. Augmented Reality (AR) is playing a key role in improving and enhancing the grocery shopping experience, both online and in-store.

AR technology introduces an immersive and interactive element to grocery shopping by overlaying digital information, visuals, and tools on top of the physical environment. This can help consumers make more informed choices, discover new products, and engage in a more personalized shopping experience. Let's explore how AR is revolutionizing grocery shopping:

1. **Enhanced Product Information**:
One of the major benefits of AR in grocery shopping is the ability to access additional product information instantly. Through an AR-enabled app, customers can scan product labels or QR codes to view detailed information such as nutritional content, sourcing, allergens, and other key features that might not be readily available on the packaging.

   o **Example**: A customer could scan the barcode of a food product and instantly see a detailed breakdown of its ingredients, calories, and even recipe suggestions.

2. **Personalized Shopping**:
AR can be used to personalize the shopping experience based on the customer's preferences, health goals, or dietary needs. By analyzing a shopper's preferences or previous purchases, AR tools can offer tailored recommendations that match their unique needs, making grocery shopping more relevant and efficient.

   o **Example**: An AR tool could suggest alternative products for customers who are gluten-free, vegan, or following other specific diets, helping them discover suitable options that they may have overlooked.

3. **Virtual Food Experiences and Recipe Tools**:
AR can also be integrated with recipe tools, allowing

customers to interact with food products and visualize how they can be combined to create meals. By superimposing digital images of ingredients and recipes into the real world, AR can help customers plan meals, find inspiration, and ensure they have all the necessary ingredients before making a purchase.

- o **Example**: An app might let customers scan an item in their kitchen and suggest recipes that incorporate that ingredient, along with a virtual display of how the dish will look when prepared.

4. **Interactive In-Store Navigation**: For physical grocery stores, AR can improve the in-store shopping experience by guiding customers to the products they need. By using AR-enabled apps, shoppers can simply point their phones at the store layout and receive real-time directions to the correct aisle or shelf where their desired products are located.

- o **Example**: If a customer is looking for a specific brand of cereal, the app can guide them directly to the aisle, saving time and enhancing the overall shopping experience.

5. **Visualizing Portions and Serving Sizes**: Another useful AR application in grocery shopping is the ability to visualize portion sizes or serving suggestions. AR can overlay digital markers on products to show the appropriate portion size, making it easier for consumers

to manage their servings, especially for health-conscious shoppers.

- **Example**: AR can show a visual representation of the correct portion of pasta, rice, or meat for a family meal, helping customers make better-informed decisions when shopping for ingredients.

Real-World Examples: Walmart's AR Shopping and Recipe Tools

Several major grocery retailers are already experimenting with and implementing AR technology to improve the customer shopping experience. Let's take a closer look at how **Walmart** is using AR to enhance the grocery shopping journey.

1. **Walmart's AR Shopping Tools**

Walmart, one of the largest retail chains in the world, has embraced AR to create a more engaging and efficient shopping experience for customers. Through **Walmart's AR-powered app**, customers can access a variety of features designed to streamline their shopping journey.

How it Works:

- **In-Store Navigation**: Walmart's AR-enabled app helps customers navigate the store by guiding them directly to the aisle or shelf where the products they're looking for are located. The app overlays digital arrows and signage on the user's screen, offering step-by-step guidance.
- **Product Scanning**: Customers can scan product barcodes using the app to access detailed information such as price, nutritional content, reviews, and even alternative product suggestions.
- **Personalized Recommendations**: Walmart's AR tools can suggest products based on a shopper's preferences or previous purchases, helping them discover new items they might like.

Impact on Customer Experience:

- **Convenience**: By offering in-store navigation and quick access to product information, Walmart's AR tools save customers time and effort during their shopping trips, making the process more convenient and efficient.
- **Increased Engagement**: The interactive and personalized nature of AR encourages customers to engage more with the store's offerings, helping to drive sales and enhance brand loyalty.
- **Reduced Decision Fatigue**: By providing tailored recommendations and detailed product information, AR helps customers make more confident purchase decisions,

reducing the frustration of indecision and the risk of making poor choices.

2. Walmart's Recipe Tools with AR

Walmart has also integrated AR into its recipe tools, enabling customers to discover new meal ideas and visualize ingredients in a more interactive way. Walmart's **Recipe Finder** app offers virtual recipe suggestions, and when paired with AR, it allows customers to visualize how certain dishes will look when made.

How it Works:

- **Recipe Visualization**: By using the app, customers can scan food products and instantly see recipe suggestions based on those ingredients. The AR tool overlays images of the completed dish, allowing customers to visualize how the final meal will look.
- **Ingredient Management**: The app can show customers what ingredients they still need to purchase and guide them to those items within the store. It ensures that customers have everything they need to prepare the dish, improving the overall shopping experience.
- **Interactive Meal Planning**: Customers can experiment with different ingredients or substitute items to create a customized recipe, visualizing each change in real-time.

Impact on Customer Experience:

- **Inspiration and Discovery**: By offering recipe suggestions and meal ideas, Walmart's AR tools inspire customers to try new dishes and explore different products, enhancing the overall grocery shopping experience.

- **Improved Shopping Efficiency**: The app helps customers manage their shopping lists more effectively, ensuring they don't forget essential ingredients and reducing the likelihood of making unnecessary trips to the store.

- **Personalization**: The ability to visualize and customize recipes based on personal preferences makes the shopping experience more relevant to the individual, encouraging repeat visits and fostering customer loyalty.

Conclusion

AR technology is significantly enhancing the grocery and food shopping experience by offering virtual product trials, personalized recommendations, and interactive features that engage customers and improve their decision-making process. Tools like **Walmart's AR shopping and recipe apps** are paving the way for more immersive, convenient, and efficient grocery shopping experiences, both online and in-store. As AR technology continues to evolve, the grocery sector will continue to benefit from these innovations, making shopping more personalized, enjoyable, and streamlined. By integrating AR into the shopping journey, retailers can meet the growing consumer demand for convenience, personalization, and engagement, driving customer satisfaction and loyalty.

CHAPTER 15

CHANGING CONSUMER EXPECTATIONS

How AR Shifts the Way Consumers Shop Online and In-Store

Augmented Reality (AR) is profoundly changing consumer behavior and expectations in both online and in-store retail environments. As AR technology becomes more integrated into shopping experiences, consumers are increasingly expecting brands to provide immersive, interactive, and personalized ways to engage with products before making a purchase. This shift is pushing retailers to rethink how they interact with customers, how they showcase products, and how they provide a seamless and enhanced shopping journey.

AR has the potential to transform traditional retail by bridging the gap between the tactile, hands-on experience of shopping in-store and the convenience of shopping online. By allowing customers to visualize and interact with products in real-time, AR elevates the shopping experience, leading to more informed purchase decisions, greater customer satisfaction, and increased brand loyalty.

Here's how AR is shifting consumer expectations and transforming shopping behavior:

1. **Expectations of Immersive and Interactive Experiences**:
   Consumers are now accustomed to the level of engagement that AR provides. Whether it's trying on makeup virtually, visualizing furniture in their living room, or testing out a pair of shoes, AR makes shopping more engaging, interactive, and fun. As a result, consumers expect brands to offer similar experiences in both physical stores and online platforms.
   - o **Example**: Customers now expect to be able to try products virtually before purchasing, whether that's through an AR try-on for apparel, an interactive furniture display, or an immersive car configurator.

2. **Desire for Personalization**:
   With AR, retailers can provide highly personalized shopping experiences by using the technology to tailor recommendations and virtual try-ons based on individual preferences, past purchases, and browsing behavior. This has raised consumer expectations for more personalized, relevant product suggestions and experiences that speak to their unique tastes and needs.
   - o **Example**: An AR-powered app that analyzes a customer's facial features and recommends

116

makeup shades or an AR configurator that suggests furniture items based on the style of the customer's existing home decor.

3. **Blending of Physical and Digital Shopping**: AR enables consumers to experience the benefits of both physical and digital shopping environments. In-store, customers can use AR tools to visualize products, while online shoppers can engage with virtual showrooms or experience real-time, interactive demonstrations. This blending of the physical and digital realms has made consumers more demanding about the kind of experiences they expect across all touchpoints.

   o **Example**: Consumers no longer want to choose between the convenience of online shopping and the tactile experience of in-store shopping; they want both. AR helps create a bridge, enabling virtual shopping experiences that mimic the physical touch and feel of a store.

4. **Need for Instant Gratification**: In the age of digital immediacy, consumers have developed a preference for instant access to information and products. AR satisfies this need by providing real-time, instant previews of products and experiences. Shoppers no longer want to wait for delivery times or spend time visiting physical stores—they want immediate

access to product visualizations, customization options, and immersive experiences.

- o **Example**: Consumers can use AR to try on clothing, see how a piece of furniture fits into their home, or experiment with makeup shades in real-time without needing to wait for physical product samples or delivery.

5. **Higher Expectations of Product Transparency and Information**:

With AR, consumers can access more detailed, transparent product information right at their fingertips. They expect to be able to explore not only the physical appearance of a product but also its features, ingredients, or technical specifications in depth. AR allows customers to make more informed decisions by providing deeper insights and context about the products they're considering.

- o **Example**: Customers can scan food products with AR to access detailed nutritional information, or they can explore the components of a piece of technology or furniture before deciding to buy.

Real-World Examples: Shift in Shopping Habits Due to AR Tech

The rise of AR technology has already influenced significant changes in shopping habits. From increased customer engagement to higher expectations of product interaction, AR is shaping consumer behavior and changing the way we shop. Let's take a closer look at how AR has shifted shopping habits through some notable examples.

1. **Sephora's Virtual Artist (Beauty)**

Sephora, a global beauty retailer, has successfully implemented AR to transform the way consumers shop for makeup. Through its **Virtual Artist** tool, customers can use AR to try on makeup products virtually before purchasing them. This tool allows customers to see how different makeup products—such as lipstick, eyeshadow, and foundation—will look on their skin tone and face in real time.

How it Shifts Consumer Expectations:

- **More Personalized Shopping**: Sephora's AR tool customizes the shopping experience by allowing users to experiment with various makeup looks, offering a highly personalized shopping experience.
- **On-Demand Engagement**: Instead of simply browsing makeup items online, customers expect to interact with the products and see how they fit their features before

making a purchase, driving the expectation of a more interactive, self-service shopping journey.

- **Instant Gratification**: Customers are no longer limited by in-store testing or waiting for samples. AR provides immediate access to try-on experiences, which aligns with consumer demand for instant access to information and experiences.

2. L'Oreal's AR Try-On Tool (Beauty)

L'Oreal has also adopted AR to enhance the beauty shopping experience with its **AR Try-On** tool. This feature allows users to virtually apply makeup products, including foundation, lipstick, and eye makeup, to their face using their smartphone or computer camera.

How it Shifts Consumer Expectations:

- **Increased Interaction**: L'Oreal's AR Try-On tool allows users to interact with the products in a way that traditional online shopping cannot. This shifts expectations toward interactive, hands-on experiences, even in a digital environment.
- **Real-Time Customization**: Consumers now expect to see how products look on them immediately, which can result in more confidence in their purchasing decisions and less hesitation.

- **Virtual Sampling**: The ability to try makeup virtually means that customers no longer feel the need to visit stores to try on products physically, which changes the way they approach beauty shopping altogether.

3. **IKEA's AR Place (Home Furnishing)**

IKEA has introduced AR technology with its **IKEA Place** app, which allows users to visualize how IKEA furniture will look and fit in their homes before making a purchase. By using their smartphones or tablets, customers can see true-to-scale 3D models of furniture in their living spaces, which helps them make decisions about size, style, and fit.

How it Shifts Consumer Expectations:

- **Virtual Showrooms**: Consumers now expect to be able to see how large items like furniture will fit in their homes before buying them, shifting expectations toward the need for virtual showrooms and product visualizations.
- **Convenience and Engagement**: With the AR tool, consumers can experiment with different furniture arrangements and styles, providing a more engaging and personalized shopping experience from the comfort of their homes.
- **Confidence and Reduced Returns**: By allowing customers to visualize how products will look in their

spaces, IKEA has reduced uncertainty, resulting in more confident purchase decisions and fewer returns.

4. Nike's AR Fitting Rooms (Fashion & Footwear)

Nike has embraced AR technology to offer customers a virtual fitting room experience for shoes. The **Nike AR Fitting Room** allows customers to scan their feet with their smartphones and virtually try on different shoe models, sizes, and styles before making a purchase.

How it Shifts Consumer Expectations:

- **Seamless Integration**: Consumers expect to easily try on shoes and other fashion items digitally, making the shopping experience more seamless and convenient, especially when it comes to footwear.
- **Enhanced Personalization**: By allowing customers to virtually try on shoes and receive recommendations, Nike personalizes the experience and aligns with the growing demand for tailored shopping journeys.
- **Hygiene and Convenience**: With the ability to try on shoes virtually, customers no longer need to physically try on multiple pairs, which enhances hygiene and provides a more efficient shopping experience.

Conclusion

The introduction of AR technology has fundamentally shifted consumer expectations in retail, especially in the areas of product interaction, personalization, and convenience. Consumers now expect to engage with products in immersive, interactive ways that bridge the gap between digital and physical shopping. Whether it's trying on makeup virtually, visualizing furniture in their homes, or configuring products to their liking, AR offers consumers a more personalized, engaging, and immediate shopping experience.

Brands like **Sephora**, **L'Oreal**, **IKEA**, and **Nike** are already meeting these new expectations by incorporating AR into their shopping platforms, helping customers make more informed decisions and enhancing overall satisfaction. As AR continues to evolve, consumers will continue to demand more seamless and interactive shopping experiences, and brands will need to adapt to these changing expectations in order to stay competitive in the retail landscape.

CHAPTER 16

THE RISE OF IMMERSIVE SHOPPING EXPERIENCES

AR's Role in Creating Immersive and Interactive Retail Environments

In the ever-evolving retail landscape, consumers are no longer satisfied with traditional, passive shopping experiences. They crave interactive, engaging, and memorable interactions with brands. As a result, Augmented Reality (AR) has become an essential tool for creating immersive shopping environments that captivate and engage customers in entirely new ways.

AR offers retailers the ability to merge the physical and digital worlds, creating environments where customers can interact with products, brands, and even the store layout itself in innovative ways. Through AR, consumers can explore virtual worlds, try on products, customize their purchases, and receive real-time recommendations, all while being physically present in the store or navigating a virtual environment online.

The rise of AR has led to a shift in how consumers experience shopping, as AR provides a layer of digital interaction that elevates the shopping journey from a simple transaction to an engaging experience. Let's explore how AR is playing a critical role in creating immersive and interactive retail environments:

1. **Immersive Store Environments**: AR can transform physical stores into interactive environments where customers engage with products in unique and creative ways. By integrating AR displays and experiences into store layouts, brands can offer a fully immersive shopping experience, where customers interact with digital elements while still physically engaging with the store.

   o **Example**: Customers can walk into a store and use their smartphones or AR glasses to interact with product displays, unlocking additional information, tutorials, or special offers as they explore the store.

2. **Interactive Product Displays**: AR enables brands to create interactive product displays that go beyond traditional signage or product tags. By overlaying digital information on physical products, retailers can provide real-time, dynamic content to educate customers about product features, specifications, and benefits. This interaction allows customers to engage with the products more deeply and make informed purchase decisions.

125

    o **Example**: A customer could point their phone at a piece of furniture to see a 3D model, view its construction process, or see how it would look in different settings.

3. **Customizable and Personalized Shopping Experiences**:

AR allows retailers to offer customized, personalized experiences that align with a customer's preferences. Whether through virtual try-ons, custom product configurations, or personalized recommendations, AR enables customers to interact with the store and products in a way that reflects their individual tastes and needs.

    o **Example**: A virtual mirror that uses AR to allow customers to try on different clothes, colors, or styles, offering tailored options based on their preferences and previous purchases.

4. **Blending of Online and In-Store Shopping**:

One of the key aspects of AR is its ability to integrate both online and offline shopping experiences. AR allows customers to enhance their in-store experience with digital elements, while also offering the convenience of online shopping. This seamless integration of physical and digital shopping has become an essential part of the modern retail experience.

    o **Example**: A customer shopping in a mall might use AR on their smartphone to navigate to a

126

specific store, scan product labels for more information, and even interact with virtual displays—all while still physically moving through the space.

5. **Enhanced Brand Engagement and Storytelling**: AR has the ability to engage consumers on an emotional level by telling compelling brand stories. Through AR, retailers can use immersive digital content to bring their brand values, history, and vision to life, creating a deeper connection between the customer and the brand.

   o **Example**: A brand could use AR to take customers on a virtual journey through the company's history, values, or production process, allowing them to interact with key moments in the brand's development.

Real-World Examples: AR in Malls, Pop-Up AR Stores

The integration of AR into retail environments has become a growing trend, with many brands and shopping centers using this technology to create unique, immersive, and engaging shopping experiences. Let's look at how AR is being used in malls and pop-up stores to revolutionize the retail experience.

1. **AR in Malls**

Malls are increasingly adopting AR technology to enhance the shopper experience and drive foot traffic. By integrating AR into their environments, shopping centers can offer interactive experiences, assist with navigation, and provide personalized recommendations.

How it Works:

- **AR Navigation**: Malls can use AR to help shoppers navigate through the complex layouts of large shopping centers. Through a mobile app or AR glasses, customers can access real-time directions to stores, find special offers, or even discover new areas of the mall they might not have noticed.
- **Interactive Displays**: Mall stores can integrate AR into their displays, allowing customers to scan QR codes or use AR apps to unlock product information, special deals, or even limited-time promotions.
- **Personalized Shopping**: By tracking shopper preferences and behavior, malls can provide personalized AR experiences, suggesting stores, products, or services that align with the customer's interests and past purchases.

Real-World Example:

- **Westfield Mall** in London: Westfield Mall implemented an AR navigation app that helps customers find their way around the large shopping complex. The app also provides interactive maps, store details, and personalized shopping recommendations, enhancing the customer's overall shopping experience.

Impact on Consumer Behavior:

- **Increased Engagement**: AR-powered mall experiences keep shoppers engaged, making their visit more enjoyable and immersive.
- **More Informed Shoppers**: By offering real-time information and personalized recommendations, AR helps shoppers make more informed decisions, improving the overall shopping journey.
- **Higher Foot Traffic**: Interactive AR experiences encourage more foot traffic, as consumers are drawn to the novelty and convenience of the technology.

2. **Pop-Up AR Stores**

Pop-up stores have long been a popular strategy for brands to create unique, temporary retail experiences. By incorporating AR technology into pop-up shops, brands can offer engaging and memorable experiences that drive consumer interest and increase sales.

How it Works:

- **Virtual Product Try-Ons**: Pop-up AR stores can offer virtual try-ons for clothing, makeup, or accessories. Customers can experiment with different looks in real-time, ensuring they make the right choice before purchasing.
- **Immersive Brand Experiences**: Pop-up stores can use AR to create immersive, interactive environments that reflect the brand's identity. This can include digital displays, 3D visualizations, or AR-enabled storytelling experiences that engage customers on a deeper level.
- **Product Customization**: AR can allow customers to customize products in real-time, whether it's selecting colors, materials, or designs, and visualize how their customizations will look before buying.

Real-World Example:

- **Kendra Scott AR Pop-Up Store**: The jewelry brand Kendra Scott has used AR technology in pop-up stores to allow customers to virtually try on various pieces of jewelry, including rings, necklaces, and bracelets. The AR tool provides a highly personalized experience, helping customers experiment with different combinations and styles before making a purchase.

- **Adidas AR Pop-Up Store**: Adidas created a pop-up AR store where customers could experience the latest shoes and clothing through augmented reality. The AR experience included virtual product displays and 3D renderings that allowed customers to explore the products from multiple angles and try on footwear virtually.

Impact on Consumer Behavior:

- **Enhanced Brand Recall**: The novelty and interactivity of AR pop-up stores leave a lasting impression on consumers, increasing brand recall and generating positive word-of-mouth.
- **Increased Sales**: By offering engaging experiences and making product interactions easier, AR pop-up stores can drive higher conversion rates and boost sales.
- **Unique Brand Experiences**: AR pop-up stores offer consumers a unique and memorable experience that stands out from the typical retail environment, enhancing customer loyalty and repeat business.

Conclusion

The rise of AR technology is fundamentally changing the way consumers engage with brands and products, creating immersive and interactive retail environments that blend the digital and physical worlds. AR is helping retailers create more personalized, engaging, and memorable shopping experiences, whether in shopping malls, pop-up stores, or online platforms. Brands that embrace AR will be better positioned to meet the growing consumer demand for innovative and convenient shopping experiences that provide both entertainment and value. As AR technology continues to evolve, it will undoubtedly play a significant role in shaping the future of retail and consumer behavior.

CHAPTER 17

AR IN CUSTOMER SERVICE AND SUPPORT

How AR Can Enhance Customer Support and Service in Retail

Customer service is a critical component of the retail experience, and as consumers increasingly expect faster, more efficient, and personalized interactions with brands, businesses are leveraging technology to meet these demands. Augmented Reality (AR) is one such technology that is revolutionizing the way brands offer customer service and support. By integrating AR into their service channels, retailers can provide customers with interactive, immersive, and real-time assistance that enhances the overall shopping experience.

AR is enhancing customer service in several key ways, enabling businesses to streamline troubleshooting, product setup, training, and technical support while providing customers with immediate, accurate solutions. Here's how AR is transforming customer service in retail:

1. **Virtual Troubleshooting and Problem-Solving**: One of the most significant ways AR can enhance customer support is through virtual troubleshooting. Instead of relying on lengthy phone calls, emails, or chat support, AR can provide step-by-step visual guides, overlaying instructions directly onto the customer's view of the product. This immediate, visual form of support allows customers to solve problems quickly and efficiently, without waiting for a technician or support representative.

   o **Example**: A customer encountering issues with a tech product can use an AR app to view step-by-step guidance for troubleshooting, such as fixing software errors, installing updates, or resolving hardware issues.

2. **Product Setup and Installation Assistance**: For products that require installation or setup, AR can provide guided, interactive instructions that help customers assemble or configure products with ease. By overlaying visual instructions or arrows in the customer's environment, AR makes the setup process simpler and more intuitive, reducing the need for customer support calls or manuals.

   o **Example**: A customer buying a new piece of furniture can use an AR app to see 3D animations

134

of how to assemble the product, with visual cues highlighting where parts fit together.

3. **Real-Time Remote Assistance**: AR can connect customers with remote experts, allowing them to receive real-time assistance while interacting with the product. Through AR-enabled devices, customers can share their view of the product with customer service representatives, who can then provide live guidance, draw on the screen, or highlight areas that need attention.

   o **Example**: If a customer experiences difficulties setting up a smart appliance, an AR-enabled video call can allow a technician to virtually guide them through the installation, with annotations or diagrams directly shown on the customer's screen.

4. **Interactive Knowledge Bases and FAQs**: AR can make traditional knowledge bases and FAQ sections more engaging and effective by providing interactive, visual explanations of common issues. Instead of sifting through text-based answers, customers can use AR to access more dynamic, step-by-step tutorials or interactive diagrams that demonstrate how to resolve common issues.

   o **Example**: Instead of reading a long FAQ article, a customer with a broken appliance can use an AR app to view a 3D diagram or video guide

135

showing how to replace a faulty part or reset the device.

5. **Personalized Customer Service**: AR can make customer service more personalized by tailoring experiences to individual needs. For example, if a customer frequently buys products from a particular category, the AR app can provide personalized product recommendations, guides, or even offer special promotions, enhancing the customer's overall experience with the brand.

   o **Example**: A customer who frequently buys home improvement tools may receive personalized AR recommendations for new tools, complete with virtual demonstrations or detailed usage instructions.

Real-World Examples: AR Troubleshooting in Tech Products

Several companies in the tech and retail sectors have adopted AR technology to improve their customer service and support, helping customers resolve issues more effectively while minimizing the need for traditional support methods. Let's look at some examples of AR in action for customer support, particularly in troubleshooting tech products.

1. IKEA's AR for Product Assembly (Furniture)

IKEA, known for its flat-packed furniture, has embraced AR to assist customers in assembling products. Through its **IKEA Place** app and **IKEA Home Smart** features, the brand has integrated AR into the customer service experience by helping users set up and assemble their furniture.

How it Works:

- **Step-by-Step Assembly**: The IKEA app overlays 3D instructions and assembly steps on the customer's real-world environment, guiding them through the process of assembling furniture. The app shows exactly where each piece should go and how they fit together.
- **Visual Troubleshooting**: If the customer encounters an issue, the AR app can help them identify where they may have gone wrong, highlighting misassembled parts and offering solutions.

Impact on Customer Experience:

- **Reduced Need for Support Calls**: By offering detailed, visual assembly instructions, IKEA reduces the number of calls customers need to make to their customer service team.

- **Increased Satisfaction**: Customers can complete the assembly on their own, reducing frustration and providing a more empowered, positive shopping experience.

2. Microsoft's AR for Tech Support (Surface Devices)

Microsoft has used AR to enhance the support experience for its **Surface** devices, offering customers interactive troubleshooting and repair assistance. Through the **Microsoft Support app**, customers can scan their device with their phone and access real-time troubleshooting tips, product guides, and even connect with a support agent if needed.

How it Works:

- **Virtual Assistance**: When a customer encounters an issue with their Surface device, they can use AR to scan the problem area or connect to an agent remotely. The agent can use AR to overlay instructions or diagnostic tools on the customer's device, helping them resolve the issue step-by-step.
- **Real-Time Troubleshooting**: If the device is malfunctioning, the app can guide the customer through real-time troubleshooting by overlaying suggestions, such as how to restart the device, clear software errors, or fix hardware issues.

Impact on Customer Experience:

138

- **Enhanced Troubleshooting**: By allowing customers to troubleshoot directly with AR instructions, Microsoft minimizes downtime for customers and enhances their experience with immediate support.

- **Convenience and Empowerment**: Customers feel more empowered to solve issues themselves with clear visual guidance, making the experience faster and more convenient.

3. **Apple's AR for Product Repairs (iPhones and iPads)**

Apple has leveraged AR to enhance its customer service for product repairs and troubleshooting. With its **Apple Support app**, Apple customers can use AR to visually diagnose issues with their devices or follow virtual repair guides to resolve minor issues without visiting an Apple Store.

How it Works:

- **AR Troubleshooting**: Using the app, customers can scan their device to receive real-time instructions for common issues like software problems, broken buttons, or connectivity issues. The AR tool overlays repair steps directly onto the customer's screen.

- **Repair and Setup Assistance**: For more complex issues, AR guides customers through product setup or directs them to the nearest Apple Store or authorized service provider.

Impact on Customer Experience:

- **Improved Self-Service**: Customers can handle many issues on their own, without needing to wait for in-person repairs, leading to a quicker resolution and less reliance on support agents.
- **Efficient Support**: AR reduces the time customers need to spend on the phone or waiting for an appointment, providing faster resolution and boosting customer satisfaction.

4. **BMW's AR for Car Troubleshooting and Maintenance**

BMW has implemented AR for troubleshooting and maintenance in its **BMW i Assistant**, which helps customers diagnose and resolve issues with their vehicles in real-time. By using AR, BMW provides a virtual assistant that overlays real-time diagnostics and guides customers through basic repairs and maintenance tasks.

How it Works:

- **Interactive Troubleshooting**: Drivers can use the BMW i Assistant app to scan their vehicle's engine or components for real-time diagnostics. The app provides step-by-step visual instructions on what to do next if the car has a problem.

- **Remote Assistance**: For more complex issues, the app can connect customers with a BMW service representative who can guide them through repairs or help them schedule an appointment.

Impact on Customer Experience:

- **Faster Issue Resolution**: AR allows customers to address minor vehicle issues quickly, without having to visit a service center.
- **Enhanced Convenience**: With real-time troubleshooting and remote assistance, BMW enhances the customer experience by providing accessible, interactive support for vehicle maintenance.

Conclusion

AR is transforming customer service in the retail and tech industries by offering real-time, interactive, and visual troubleshooting and assistance. By reducing the need for traditional customer service channels, AR empowers consumers to resolve issues independently and efficiently, improving satisfaction and reducing wait times. Brands like **IKEA**, **Microsoft**, **Apple**, and **BMW** are already leveraging AR to enhance their customer support services, offering interactive troubleshooting, product setup assistance, and personalized support experiences. As AR technology continues to evolve, it will become an increasingly integral part of customer service, further elevating the customer experience and meeting the growing demand for fast, effective, and personalized solutions.

CHAPTER 18

BUILDING BRAND AWARENESS AND LOYALTY WITH AR

How Brands Are Using AR to Increase Recognition and Customer Retention

In the competitive world of retail, brand awareness and customer loyalty are crucial to long-term success. Companies are always seeking new ways to differentiate themselves from competitors, engage consumers in meaningful ways, and keep them coming back for more. Augmented Reality (AR) has emerged as an innovative and effective tool to build brand recognition and increase customer retention. By offering immersive, interactive experiences, brands are leveraging AR to captivate consumers and create deeper emotional connections.

AR's ability to merge the physical and digital worlds provides opportunities for brands to deliver unique, memorable, and personalized experiences that leave lasting impressions. These experiences help customers form stronger relationships with brands, resulting in increased brand awareness and greater customer loyalty.

Here's how AR can help brands build awareness and retain loyal customers:

1. **Engaging and Memorable Experiences**: AR allows brands to create memorable experiences that go beyond traditional advertising or promotional tactics. By offering something new, fun, and engaging, brands can capture the attention of consumers, creating a positive association with the brand. These interactive and immersive experiences are often shared on social media, amplifying brand exposure and recognition.

   o **Example**: An AR app that allows users to virtually try on products or explore interactive brand experiences can create a memorable moment that encourages customers to engage with the brand more deeply.

2. **Personalization and Customization**: AR can help brands deliver highly personalized experiences based on individual customer preferences, past purchases, or browsing behavior. By offering customized product recommendations or virtual try-ons, brands can make customers feel valued and understood, fostering loyalty and repeat business.

   o **Example**: Brands that allow customers to personalize their product choices or customize features using AR tools can create a sense of ownership and connection to the brand.

144

3. **Incorporating   Gamification**:
   AR opens up the potential for gamification, turning shopping or brand interactions into fun, rewarding experiences. Brands can create challenges, contests, or scavenger hunts that involve AR, motivating customers to engage with the brand and return for more interactions.

   o **Example**: Customers might participate in an AR scavenger hunt where they unlock exclusive rewards, promotions, or discounts as they engage with different brand touchpoints.

4. **Interactive   and   Engaging   Advertising**:
   Traditional advertisements can sometimes feel passive, but AR takes advertising to a new level by offering interactive and engaging elements that captivate the audience. AR advertisements allow customers to interact with the ad, explore 3D models of products, or even trigger immersive brand stories that draw consumers in.

   o **Example**: An AR ad that allows users to interact with a product in 3D, see how it fits in their environment, or participate in a branded AR experience can drive higher engagement and foster positive associations with the brand.

5. **Seamless Integration of AR Across Channels**:
   AR can be seamlessly integrated into various touchpoints, whether online or in-store. Whether through a mobile app, social media filters, or in-store AR experiences,

consumers can engage with the brand wherever they are, creating consistent and meaningful interactions that build trust and loyalty.

- o **Example**: A brand can offer an AR experience both in-store (e.g., scanning a product to see additional features) and online (e.g., trying on clothes virtually), ensuring a consistent experience across multiple channels.

Real-World Examples: AR Experiences in Advertising (Gucci, Coca-Cola)

Several leading brands are already using AR to create interactive advertising experiences that boost brand awareness, engage customers, and drive loyalty. Let's take a closer look at how **Gucci** and **Coca-Cola** have incorporated AR into their advertising strategies:

1. **Gucci: AR Try-On Experience (Fashion)**

Gucci, the luxury fashion brand, has embraced AR to revolutionize how customers interact with their products. Gucci's AR-powered **try-on experience** allows customers to virtually try on their shoes using a smartphone or tablet, creating a personalized and immersive shopping experience.

146

How it Works:

- **Virtual Try-On**: Using the **Gucci app**, customers can scan their feet with their phone's camera and virtually try on various shoe styles in real-time. The AR tool projects a 3D image of the shoes onto the user's feet, allowing them to see how the shoes look from different angles.
- **Interactive Shopping**: The app allows users to interact with the shoes, view product details, and even share images of their virtual try-ons with friends on social media, increasing brand visibility and engagement.

Impact on Brand Awareness and Loyalty:

- **Increased Engagement**: The AR try-on experience engages customers by allowing them to interact with the brand in a fun and personalized way. This increases the likelihood of customers sharing their experiences, generating organic brand awareness through social media.
- **Memorable Experiences**: By offering an immersive, high-tech shopping experience, Gucci stands out from other luxury brands and creates lasting, positive memories for customers, fostering brand loyalty.
- **Cross-Channel Interaction**: The AR experience bridges the gap between online and offline shopping, allowing customers to engage with the brand both in-store and

online, providing a seamless and cohesive brand experience.

2. Coca-Cola: AR Advertising Campaigns

Coca-Cola, one of the most recognized global brands, has used AR to create engaging and interactive advertising campaigns that build brand recognition and drive consumer engagement. Coca-Cola has experimented with AR in several campaigns, including its **AR-enabled cans**, which provide consumers with a fun, interactive experience through their smartphones.

How it Works:

- **AR-Enabled Cans**: Coca-Cola launched special edition cans with **AR codes** printed on them. When customers scanned the code with their smartphones, they unlocked interactive experiences, such as games, virtual animations, or brand stories.
- **Interactive Branding**: Coca-Cola used AR to bring the brand to life in a unique, fun way, creating memorable moments that connected with customers emotionally and encouraged them to engage with the brand.

Impact on Brand Awareness and Loyalty:

- **Engaging Advertising**: By integrating AR into their advertising campaigns, Coca-Cola transformed

148

traditional packaging into an interactive experience that encouraged customers to connect with the brand on a deeper level.

- **Emotional Connection**: The AR experiences evoked positive emotions, such as excitement or nostalgia, which helped build a strong emotional connection with the brand, increasing customer loyalty.
- **Wider Brand Reach**: AR-enabled cans generated excitement and curiosity, leading to greater brand exposure and social sharing as customers posted their AR experiences online, amplifying the campaign's reach.

3. **L'Oréal: AR in Beauty Ads**

L'Oréal has integrated AR into its advertising to enhance the shopping experience for beauty consumers. Through its **AR makeup try-on technology**, L'Oréal allows consumers to experiment with different makeup products and looks directly from their smartphones or computers, providing an immersive experience.

How it Works:

- **Virtual Try-Ons**: L'Oréal uses AR to allow users to virtually try on various makeup products like lipstick, foundation, and eyeshadow. Customers can see how different shades will look on their skin tone before making a purchase.

- **Interactive Ads**: L'Oréal has incorporated AR features into its advertising campaigns, offering interactive beauty tutorials and virtual try-on ads to engage customers in an interactive and personalized manner.

Impact on Brand Awareness and Loyalty:

- **Customer Engagement**: The ability to try on products virtually directly through ads drives greater engagement, making the experience more enjoyable and interactive.
- **Brand Recall**: By offering an immersive experience, L'Oréal's AR campaigns leave a lasting impression, increasing brand recall and consumer loyalty.
- **Seamless Integration**: L'Oréal integrates AR into both its online and offline marketing, creating a consistent experience that bridges the gap between the digital and physical worlds, further enhancing brand loyalty.

Conclusion

AR is playing a key role in increasing brand awareness and customer loyalty by offering innovative, interactive, and personalized experiences. Through AR, brands like **Gucci**, **Coca-Cola**, and **L'Oréal** are engaging consumers in new and exciting ways, transforming traditional advertising into immersive experiences that captivate and retain customers. As AR continues to evolve, brands will have even more opportunities to leverage this technology to create meaningful connections, enhance customer satisfaction, and drive long-term loyalty. By using AR to make shopping and brand interactions more engaging, brands can differentiate themselves in a competitive market and build lasting relationships with their customers.

CHAPTER 19

AR'S ROLE IN ENHANCING SOCIAL COMMERCE

How AR Contributes to Social Media-Driven Commerce

Social commerce, the intersection of social media and e-commerce, has become a dominant force in the retail industry. With the rise of platforms like Instagram, Facebook, TikTok, and Snapchat, consumers are increasingly discovering and purchasing products directly through social media channels. Augmented Reality (AR) has become a crucial tool in enhancing social commerce by creating engaging, interactive, and immersive shopping experiences that resonate with today's digital-native shoppers.

AR contributes to social commerce by enabling consumers to interact with products in fun and creative ways, increasing engagement, building emotional connections, and driving purchases. Through AR, brands can create virtual try-ons, interactive product demos, and personalized experiences that make shopping on social platforms more enjoyable and effective. Here's how AR is reshaping social commerce:

152

1. **Enhancing Shopping with Virtual Try-Ons**: AR allows consumers to try on products virtually through social media platforms, eliminating the need to visit a store physically. This is especially valuable for products like clothing, makeup, and accessories. By offering virtual try-ons, brands can create immersive shopping experiences that increase confidence in purchasing decisions.

   o **Example**: On Instagram, users can try on makeup products or sunglasses using AR filters, allowing them to see how these items would look in real-time before buying them.

2. **Interactive Product Demonstrations**: AR can turn product demonstrations into interactive experiences, allowing users to see how products work, their features, and how they will fit into their lives. This is especially useful for demonstrating complex products, new technologies, or unique product features in a way that static images or videos cannot.

   o **Example**: Brands can use AR to allow consumers to visualize how a piece of furniture would look in their living room or how a tech gadget operates, making the product experience more engaging and tangible.

3. **User-Generated Content and Social Engagement**: Social media is powered by user-generated content, and

153

AR enhances this by encouraging users to share their experiences with products. Whether it's a virtual try-on, a creative AR filter, or an interactive product demo, AR-driven content is highly shareable, helping brands reach a wider audience and increase brand visibility.

- o **Example**: Snapchat filters that allow users to try on clothes, accessories, or makeup encourage social sharing. When users post their AR-enhanced experiences, they not only engage with the brand but also help amplify its reach through their social networks.

4. **Gamification and AR-Driven Challenges**: AR can be integrated into social commerce through gamification, where users participate in challenges, games, or interactive campaigns that encourage them to engage with a brand or product. Gamified AR experiences motivate consumers to interact with products in fun and rewarding ways, often leading to purchases or deeper brand engagement.

- o **Example**: Instagram and Snapchat often feature AR challenges or games where users can "unlock" rewards, discounts, or exclusive products after completing certain tasks or engaging with branded AR filters.

5. **Creating Personalized and Engaging Brand Experiences**:

AR allows brands to personalize the shopping experience for individual users by tailoring filters, recommendations, or virtual try-ons based on their preferences, previous interactions, or browsing history. Personalization increases customer engagement and the likelihood of a purchase.

- o **Example**: A fashion brand may use AR to recommend personalized clothing items based on a user's past purchases or preferences, creating a more customized and targeted shopping experience.

Real-World Examples: Instagram Filters, Snapchat Shopping

Several social media platforms are already integrating AR into their commerce features, allowing brands to create interactive and personalized shopping experiences. Let's take a closer look at how **Instagram** and **Snapchat** are using AR to enhance social commerce and drive consumer engagement:

1. **Instagram Filters (Beauty, Fashion, Retail)**

Instagram has become a powerful platform for social commerce, with AR filters being an essential part of the shopping experience. Instagram filters allow users to try on products virtually, interact with brand content, and make shopping more fun and engaging.

155

How it Works:

- **AR Try-Ons**: Beauty brands like **Sephora** and **L'Oreal** use Instagram's AR filters to allow users to virtually try on makeup products such as lipsticks, foundation, and eyeshadows. Users can see how different shades will look on their face in real-time, encouraging them to make more informed purchase decisions.

- **Interactive Shopping**: Instagram allows users to click on products featured in AR filters, taking them directly to the product page for easy purchase. This creates a seamless path from engagement to conversion.

Impact on Social Commerce:

- **Increased Engagement**: AR filters encourage users to interact with brand content in a playful and personal way. When users share their virtual try-ons on their feeds or Stories, it increases brand exposure and encourages others to engage with the brand.

- **Boosted Sales**: By allowing users to try products virtually and then purchase them directly through Instagram's shopping features, brands can drive higher conversion rates and sales.

- **Brand Awareness**: User-generated content featuring AR filters increases brand visibility as consumers share their experiences with their followers, driving organic reach and engagement.

2. Snapchat Shopping (Fashion, Retail, Electronics)

Snapchat has long been a leader in AR innovation, with its various AR filters and lenses offering users an interactive and fun way to engage with brands and products. Snapchat has embraced AR to transform its platform into a hub for social commerce, allowing brands to integrate shopping directly into the user experience.

How it Works:

- **AR Shopping Lenses**: Snapchat has developed AR shopping lenses that allow users to try on fashion items, makeup, and accessories virtually. Brands like **Gucci**, **Ray-Ban**, and **Nike** have integrated AR lenses that let users see how products will look on them before purchasing.

- **Seamless Shopping Integration**: Users can swipe up on a product featured in an AR lens to access detailed product information, pricing, and a direct link to purchase. Snapchat also allows users to shop directly within the app, making it easy to transition from AR engagement to actual purchase.

Impact on Social Commerce:

157

- **Interactive and Fun Shopping**: Snapchat's AR lenses create a highly engaging, fun shopping experience. By allowing users to try on products virtually, the platform encourages them to interact with brands in a more dynamic and personalized way.

- **Personalized Recommendations**: Snapchat's shopping lenses are often tailored to users' preferences, making product recommendations more relevant and appealing. This increases the likelihood of conversions as users engage with products they are genuinely interested in.

- **Enhanced Brand Engagement**: The integration of AR shopping lenses with Snapchat's social features means that users can easily share their virtual try-ons with their friends and followers, amplifying brand reach and driving organic engagement.

3. **L'Oréal AR Shopping on Instagram and Snapchat (Beauty)**

L'Oréal has leveraged both Instagram and Snapchat to create AR-driven beauty shopping experiences. Through these platforms, L'Oréal has been able to offer consumers virtual try-ons for makeup, skincare, and hair products, driving engagement and brand loyalty.

How it Works:

- **Virtual Try-Ons**: L'Oréal uses AR filters on Instagram and Snapchat to allow users to try on makeup products virtually. Customers can experiment with different lipsticks, eyeshadows, and foundation shades, all while receiving real-time feedback and product recommendations.
- **Social Integration**: L'Oréal encourages users to share their virtual makeup looks on their social media, helping the brand reach a wider audience through user-generated content.

Impact on Social Commerce:

- **Increased Engagement**: By providing interactive and personalized virtual try-ons, L'Oréal enhances engagement with its audience, encouraging users to interact with the brand in a fun and personalized way.
- **Seamless Shopping Experience**: Users can click on the AR filter to shop for the makeup products they are trying on, streamlining the path from discovery to purchase.
- **Brand Loyalty**: The ability to engage with the brand in an interactive and personal way strengthens customer loyalty, as users feel more connected to the brand.

Conclusion

AR is playing a pivotal role in enhancing social commerce by creating interactive, engaging, and personalized shopping experiences. Platforms like **Instagram** and **Snapchat** are integrating AR into their shopping features, allowing consumers to virtually try on products, interact with branded content, and make seamless purchases. These AR-driven experiences not only increase brand awareness and engagement but also contribute to higher conversion rates and customer retention. As AR technology continues to evolve, it will become an even more integral part of social commerce, transforming how consumers shop and how brands connect with their audiences on social media.

CHAPTER 20

COST OF AR IMPLEMENTATION

Understanding the Cost Structure for Integrating AR into an E-Commerce Business

Integrating Augmented Reality (AR) into an e-commerce business offers incredible potential for enhancing the customer experience, increasing engagement, and driving sales. However, like any advanced technology, the implementation of AR comes with associated costs that businesses must consider. These costs can vary greatly depending on several factors, including the scale of the project, the complexity of the AR experience, and the resources available to the business.

In this chapter, we'll break down the typical cost structure of implementing AR in e-commerce, from initial development and design to ongoing maintenance and updates. Additionally, we'll explore the budget considerations for both small and medium-sized enterprises (SMEs) and large corporations, highlighting the differences in resources and strategies for adopting AR technology.

Cost Structure for AR Integration

When considering the integration of AR into an e-commerce platform, businesses should account for several key cost components. These can be categorized into **development costs**, **hardware and software costs**, **ongoing maintenance**, and **marketing and deployment costs**.

1. Development Costs

Development is the most significant and upfront cost for implementing AR technology. The process typically involves designing AR experiences, developing custom solutions, and testing the technology. Here are some key factors that contribute to development costs:

- **Custom AR Content**: Creating AR models of products, designing immersive virtual environments, and developing interactive features are all part of the initial development. Depending on the complexity and quality of the experience, costs can range from basic AR experiences to highly advanced, 3D visualizations.
- **AR Software Development**: Businesses often need specialized AR developers to build applications or integrate AR functionalities with existing e-commerce platforms. This includes coding, testing, and debugging the AR app or feature.

162

- **Platform Integration**: If the business already has an existing e-commerce platform (like Shopify, WooCommerce, or Magento), integrating AR might require additional software development to ensure compatibility with the platform. For instance, adding AR capabilities to product pages or creating a custom AR shopping experience may need specific APIs or plugins.

- **Example**: A fashion retailer seeking to build a virtual try-on feature for clothing or accessories will need 3D models of their product range, realistic lighting, and motion-tracking capabilities. This is an intensive process that involves not only graphic design but also backend infrastructure to ensure seamless operation.

2. Hardware and Software Costs

The hardware and software required to deploy AR experiences can also add significant costs. These costs can differ based on whether AR is primarily mobile-based, desktop-based, or requires specialized AR hardware.

- **Software Tools and Platforms**: Depending on the type of AR solution, businesses may need to purchase or license AR development platforms such as **Unity**, **ARKit** (for iOS), or **ARCore** (for Android). Many of these platforms offer free versions, but advanced features typically require premium licenses.

- **AR-enabled Devices**: For AR experiences that require specialized hardware, such as AR glasses or headsets, the costs will be higher. While mobile-based AR experiences can be accessed via smartphones or tablets, certain applications, like immersive product visualizations in a 3D environment, may require devices like **Microsoft HoloLens** or **Magic Leap**.

- **Example**: A small business opting to use smartphones for an AR-based shopping experience may incur relatively lower costs. In contrast, a company aiming for high-quality, immersive AR experiences may need to invest in more advanced AR hardware and a larger team of developers.

3. Ongoing Maintenance and Updates

Maintaining AR technology is a continuous cost that businesses need to factor in. AR experiences, like any other software, require regular updates, bug fixes, and improvements to keep the technology running smoothly and to ensure compatibility with new mobile devices or operating system versions.

- **Bug Fixes and Performance Optimizations**: Over time, users may encounter bugs or performance issues, particularly if new versions of the app or platform introduce compatibility challenges. Regular updates and troubleshooting are essential for maintaining a seamless AR experience.

- **Content Updates**: As products in an e-commerce catalog change, businesses will need to update their AR content to reflect these changes, including new product designs, features, or discontinued items.

- **Example**: A retailer offering AR-powered virtual try-ons will need to update their AR models regularly as new styles and product lines are introduced. This means ongoing investment in the content development process.

4. Marketing and Deployment Costs

Once the AR experience is developed and tested, it's important to promote it effectively to customers. Marketing campaigns for AR-powered features can add additional costs to the implementation. Furthermore, businesses may need to allocate resources to ensure proper deployment and integration across different digital channels.

- **Promotions and Advertising**: To generate awareness and engagement with the new AR feature, businesses may invest in social media campaigns, influencer partnerships, or paid advertisements targeting specific customer segments.

- **User Education and Support**: Since AR technology is still relatively new to many consumers, brands may need to provide tutorials, demonstrations, or customer support to help users understand how to interact with AR features.

- **Example**: A luxury brand might leverage influencer marketing to showcase their AR shopping experience. This helps drive awareness and adoption, but comes at the cost of hiring influencers, running ad campaigns, and supporting customers with how-to guides and customer service.

Budget Considerations for SMEs vs. Large Corporations

When it comes to budgeting for AR implementation, small and medium-sized enterprises (SMEs) and large corporations face different challenges and opportunities.

Small and Medium-Sized Enterprises (SMEs)

For SMEs, the key challenges with AR implementation often revolve around cost constraints and limited technical resources. However, there are ways that smaller businesses can implement AR without breaking the bank:

- **Affordable AR Solutions**: SMEs can turn to AR solutions that are already available through platforms like

Shopify AR, **Adobe Aero**, or **Wikitude**, which provide more cost-effective tools to integrate AR into e-commerce sites without needing a team of developers.

- **Smaller Scale**: Instead of investing in highly complex AR experiences, SMEs can start by implementing basic AR features like virtual try-ons for products or product demonstrations, which are relatively easier and less costly to deploy.

- **Outsourcing Development**: SMEs can also partner with third-party AR development agencies to keep costs down rather than hiring in-house teams. Many agencies offer flexible pricing models based on the scale of the project.

- **Example**: A small beauty retailer might integrate AR filters on Instagram and Snapchat to offer virtual makeup try-ons. By using existing AR technologies provided by social media platforms, they can deliver an AR experience at a fraction of the cost of developing a custom AR app.

Large Corporations

Large corporations typically have more financial resources, which allows them to implement advanced AR solutions at a larger scale. However, the complexity and scope of the project will also drive up the cost.

- **Custom AR Solutions**: Large companies often require custom-built AR solutions tailored to their specific needs.

167

This includes investing in 3D modeling, custom app development, and robust integration with existing e-commerce platforms.

- **Cross-Platform Integration**: Large corporations may need to develop AR experiences that are consistent across multiple platforms, including mobile apps, websites, and in-store experiences. This adds to the overall cost, but ensures a seamless experience for customers.

- **Scalability**: Corporations can scale AR projects to serve millions of users globally. They can invest in high-end AR hardware, larger development teams, and significant marketing budgets to promote their AR features.

- **Example: Nike** invested in creating a comprehensive AR-powered app for their customers, offering virtual try-ons, personalized recommendations, and AR product displays. This large-scale implementation required significant investment in app development, marketing, and ongoing updates.

Conclusion

The cost of implementing AR in e-commerce can vary widely depending on factors like the complexity of the AR experience, the scale of the business, and the resources available. For SMEs, there are more affordable and simple AR solutions, while large corporations can afford to create more advanced, custom-built AR experiences. Both small businesses and large enterprises should carefully evaluate the costs and benefits of integrating AR into their e-commerce strategies, keeping in mind the long-term value of increased customer engagement, satisfaction, and sales.

Ultimately, AR provides businesses of all sizes with the opportunity to enhance their customer experience, drive innovation, and stand out in a competitive retail landscape. With the right investment and strategy, the implementation of AR can pay off by creating more immersive, engaging, and efficient shopping experiences that foster brand loyalty and growth.

CHAPTER 21

TECHNICAL AND DESIGN CHALLENGES

Addressing the Technical Barriers to Creating a Seamless AR Experience

While Augmented Reality (AR) holds immense potential to revolutionize e-commerce and enhance customer experiences, implementing AR comes with its own set of technical and design challenges. Creating a seamless and effective AR experience requires overcoming several barriers, including hardware limitations, software integration, user interface design, and ensuring cross-platform compatibility. These challenges must be addressed in order to provide customers with a smooth, immersive, and enjoyable shopping experience.

This chapter will explore the technical and design obstacles that businesses face when integrating AR into e-commerce, and how they can overcome these barriers to create a high-quality, seamless AR experience for customers.

1. Hardware Limitations

Challenge:

One of the primary barriers to creating seamless AR experiences is the reliance on hardware. While smartphones and tablets have become the primary devices for AR experiences, not all devices are equally capable of delivering high-quality AR. Older devices may lack the necessary processing power, camera capabilities, or sensors to run AR apps effectively, which can result in poor performance or a subpar user experience.

Additionally, more advanced AR experiences, such as immersive 3D visualizations, may require specialized hardware like AR glasses or headsets (e.g., Microsoft HoloLens or Magic Leap), which are not yet widely adopted by consumers.

Solutions:

- **Optimizing for a Range of Devices**: Companies should ensure their AR experiences are optimized for a range of devices, balancing high-quality visuals with the technical constraints of different hardware. This means designing AR content that works smoothly on smartphones, tablets, and, in some cases, more advanced devices.
- **Mobile-First Strategy**: Since smartphones are the most widely used device for AR, focusing on optimizing AR experiences for mobile devices ensures that brands can

171

reach a broader audience. This involves simplifying graphics and utilizing device-specific AR platforms (e.g., ARKit for iOS and ARCore for Android) to ensure optimal performance.

- **Progressive Web AR**: For greater accessibility, brands can also invest in Progressive Web AR (PWAR), which allows AR experiences to be accessed through a browser, reducing the need for dedicated apps and minimizing device dependency.

Example:

When **L'Oreal** launched its AR try-on tool, it faced challenges ensuring the app worked smoothly across various phone models, especially older devices with weaker processing capabilities. To resolve this, they had to optimize their AR features to run efficiently on lower-spec devices while still providing a high-quality experience for users with advanced smartphones.

2. Software Integration and Compatibility

Challenge:

Integrating AR technology with existing e-commerce platforms and third-party tools can be a complicated and costly process. E-commerce websites and mobile apps are often built on different platforms and software, and integrating AR seamlessly into these systems requires both technical expertise and time.

For example, ensuring AR works well on popular e-commerce platforms like Shopify, Magento, or WooCommerce may require specific plugins, APIs, and custom coding. Cross-platform integration between mobile apps, websites, and AR systems can create compatibility challenges, especially when considering device-specific differences, such as screen sizes, operating systems, and processing power.

Solutions:

- **Using AR Development Platforms**: Platforms like **Unity**, **Vuforia**, and **ARKit** (for iOS) or **ARCore** (for Android) offer pre-built solutions and SDKs (software development kits) that make it easier to integrate AR experiences into existing systems. These platforms provide the necessary frameworks and tools to build AR features while minimizing the complexity of custom development.
- **Collaboration with E-Commerce Providers**: Many e-commerce platforms now offer AR integration as part of their built-in solutions. Shopify, for instance, has an **AR-enabled shopping experience** that allows businesses to create product visualizations without requiring complex coding or custom solutions.

Example:

Warby Parker, a popular eyewear brand, faced challenges when integrating AR try-on features into their website and mobile app. They used AR development platforms like **Vuforia** to simplify the integration process, but ensuring that the feature worked smoothly across different devices, operating systems, and browsers took significant effort.

3. User Interface (UI) and User Experience (UX) Design

Challenge:

AR can offer rich, interactive experiences, but it also introduces challenges in designing an intuitive and user-friendly interface. AR interactions require clear visual cues and guidance to ensure that users can easily navigate the experience without feeling overwhelmed or confused.

Creating a seamless UX for AR involves understanding how users interact with the digital world, as well as ensuring that AR content is appropriately aligned with the real world. Poorly designed UI elements, such as cluttered interfaces or unclear instructions, can ruin the immersive nature of AR, leading to frustration and abandonment.

Solutions:

- **Simplified User Flows**: In AR, the user interface should be minimalistic and intuitive. Too many options or cluttered screens can detract from the immersive experience. The goal is to make the AR experience feel natural and easy to use, without overwhelming the user.

- **Clear Instructions and Visual Cues**: Providing clear visual cues and step-by-step instructions helps users understand how to interact with AR elements. This is especially important for beginners who may not be familiar with AR technology.

- **Testing and Iteration**: Continuous user testing and iteration are essential for fine-tuning the UX and UI of AR features. Brands should gather feedback from users to identify pain points and improve the overall design.

Example:

Sephora's Virtual Artist faced challenges in designing a user-friendly interface for their AR-powered makeup try-on tool. By simplifying the interface and focusing on clear, intuitive steps, Sephora was able to enhance the user experience, ensuring that customers could easily explore makeup products without feeling overwhelmed by too many options.

175

4. Real-Time Tracking and Accuracy

Challenge:

Accurate tracking of physical objects and real-world environments is one of the most critical aspects of AR. Whether it's visualizing how a piece of furniture fits in a room or enabling virtual try-ons for apparel, ensuring that the AR system correctly tracks the user's movements and accurately displays the digital content in the correct context is essential. Poor tracking or inaccurate 3D rendering can lead to a frustrating user experience and reduced engagement.

Solutions:

- **Improving Camera and Sensor Capabilities**: AR relies heavily on the camera, sensors, and accelerometers of the device. Ensuring that AR experiences work well across a wide range of devices requires sophisticated tracking algorithms that can compensate for limitations in lower-end devices.

- **Real-Time Rendering Optimization**: To maintain smooth, realistic AR visuals, rendering must be optimized for real-time performance. This includes adjusting the level of detail and complexity of 3D models, ensuring that the experience remains responsive and immersive.

Example:

IKEA Place, which allows users to visualize furniture in their homes via AR, encountered difficulties with real-time tracking accuracy, especially in rooms with complex layouts or insufficient lighting. IKEA worked on improving the tracking algorithms and ARCore/ARKit compatibility to enhance the realism and accuracy of the AR visuals, ensuring that products appeared correctly within the user's environment.

5. Network and Data Usage Considerations

Challenge:

AR experiences often require large amounts of data, especially for high-quality 3D visuals or video streams. Consumers accessing AR experiences on mobile networks may face data usage issues, especially if they are using limited or slow network connections. This can result in slow load times, buffering, or poor-quality visuals, which can frustrate users and lead to abandonment of the AR experience.

Solutions:

- **Optimized Content Delivery**: Brands should optimize AR content to minimize data usage, using compressed textures, models, and assets to improve load times and reduce data requirements. For example, 3D models can be simplified without sacrificing key details, and textures can be compressed for faster delivery.

- **Offline Capabilities**: For certain types of AR experiences, it may be beneficial to enable offline functionality, allowing users to access certain features even when they don't have an active internet connection. This can be especially important for retail environments where internet access may be limited or unreliable.

Example:

During the launch of its **AR Try-On feature** for makeup, **L'Oréal** faced challenges with users on slow mobile networks. By optimizing the app's performance and reducing data usage, L'Oréal was able to ensure that users had a smooth experience even in areas with poor network connectivity.

Conclusion

Implementing AR in e-commerce presents several technical and design challenges that need to be addressed in order to create a seamless, engaging, and high-quality experience for customers. These challenges range from hardware limitations and software integration to UI/UX design, real-time tracking accuracy, and data usage concerns. Overcoming these obstacles requires a combination of advanced AR development tools, continuous testing and iteration, and a focus on optimizing user experience across a variety of devices and platforms.

As more businesses adopt AR in their e-commerce strategies, the technology will continue to evolve, and solutions to these challenges will become more refined. By addressing the technical barriers early on, businesses can ensure that they create a smooth, immersive, and enjoyable AR shopping experience that enhances customer satisfaction and drives sales.

CHAPTER 22

USER ADOPTION AND ACCESSIBILITY

The Challenges of Ensuring Broad Consumer Adoption and Overcoming Technological Barriers

While Augmented Reality (AR) offers immense potential for enhancing e-commerce and customer experiences, the widespread adoption of AR faces several challenges. Despite the growth of mobile-based AR technologies, many consumers are still unfamiliar with the technology, and a significant portion of the population may not have access to the required devices or networks. For businesses looking to integrate AR into their e-commerce platforms, ensuring broad consumer adoption and overcoming technological barriers is key to achieving long-term success.

In this chapter, we will explore the challenges businesses face in driving AR adoption among consumers, how to make AR more accessible across various devices, and the real-world considerations that come with overcoming these barriers.

1. Technological Barriers to AR Adoption

Challenge:

The most significant technological barrier to AR adoption is device compatibility. While modern smartphones and tablets have become more capable of supporting AR experiences, many older devices may not have the necessary hardware or software to run AR applications effectively. These devices may lack advanced cameras, sensors, or sufficient processing power, making the AR experience either unavailable or subpar.

Furthermore, specialized AR hardware such as **AR glasses** (e.g., **Microsoft HoloLens** or **Magic Leap**) are still relatively expensive and not widely adopted. While the use of AR in smartphones has become more mainstream, many consumers are still unfamiliar with AR technology, and the user experience can be inconsistent across different device types.

Solutions:

- **Optimizing for Mobile Devices**: Since smartphones and tablets are the most common devices for AR, brands should focus on optimizing their AR experiences for these devices, ensuring that the app or feature works across a broad range of models with different hardware capabilities. Platforms like **ARCore** (Android) and

181

ARKit (iOS) provide frameworks to ensure that AR experiences can run smoothly across various devices.

- **Increased Use of Web-Based AR**: To address device limitations, **web-based AR** (also known as **WebAR**) allows users to access AR experiences directly through their browser without needing to download an app. This eliminates the need for specialized hardware and increases accessibility for all users, regardless of the device they own.

Example:

Sephora's AR virtual try-on tools, available via its mobile app, have been optimized to work on a wide range of smartphones, ensuring users with different devices can still enjoy the AR experience. However, the company has also addressed accessibility concerns by offering a **WebAR** experience on its website for users who prefer not to download the app, expanding its reach beyond mobile app users.

2. User Awareness and Education

Challenge:

Many consumers are still unfamiliar with AR technology, and there is a learning curve involved in adopting this new way of shopping. AR requires users to interact with their devices in a different manner than traditional shopping experiences. For example, they may need to move their phone around to scan a product, visualize it in 3D, or interact with it virtually, which can be intimidating for new users or those not comfortable with technology.

Solutions:

- **Clear Instructions and Onboarding**: To facilitate smoother user adoption, businesses can include clear, concise instructions and tutorials that explain how to use AR features. This can include visual guides, in-app prompts, and tutorial videos that walk users through the AR experience step by step.
- **Incentivizing First-Time Use**: Offering incentives such as discounts, rewards, or exclusive promotions can motivate first-time users to try out the AR experience, making them more likely to engage with the feature and return for future purchases.

Example:

Warby Parker, the eyewear brand, introduced an AR tool for virtual try-ons, but they recognized that many customers were unfamiliar with this type of feature. To address this, they incorporated simple onboarding tutorials within the app, guiding users on how to try on glasses using their camera and navigate through the virtual experience. They also highlighted the feature in email campaigns to build awareness and encourage usage.

---

3. AR Accessibility on Various Devices (Smartphones, Tablets, and Beyond)

Challenge:

As AR continues to evolve, businesses must ensure that their AR experiences are accessible to a wide range of devices. While smartphones and tablets are the most common devices used for AR, the quality and performance of AR experiences can vary depending on the model, brand, and specifications of the device. Additionally, some users may not have access to the latest devices, limiting their ability to engage with AR-powered e-commerce features.

Solutions:

- **Device-Agnostic Solutions**: Developing AR solutions that are device-agnostic—meaning they can function across a variety of devices—is essential for broad consumer adoption. AR platforms like **ARKit** and **ARCore** provide tools that help developers ensure their AR apps are compatible with a wide range of smartphones and tablets, making it easier for businesses to reach a larger audience.

- **Support for Lower-End Devices**: While high-end devices offer the best AR experiences, businesses can optimize their AR applications for lower-end devices by simplifying graphics, reducing the complexity of AR models, and optimizing performance to ensure that the experience is still enjoyable even on less powerful smartphones.

Example:

IKEA Place, the AR-powered furniture app, is optimized to work across both high-end and budget smartphones. While it provides high-quality 3D renderings on premium devices, the app also offers simplified visuals on lower-end devices, ensuring that all users, regardless of the device they own, can access and enjoy the experience.

4. Internet and Connectivity Requirements

Challenge:

AR experiences often require a stable and fast internet connection, especially if the app uses cloud computing to render complex 3D models or stream real-time AR content. In areas with poor connectivity, users may experience lag, buffering, or crashes, which can significantly hinder their experience and lead to frustration.

Solutions:

- **Optimizing for Offline Use**: To address issues with connectivity, businesses can design AR experiences that work offline or with minimal internet usage. By preloading 3D models or assets, brands can ensure that the app functions even in low or no-network conditions.
- **Low-Data Mode**: For consumers in areas with limited or slow internet speeds, providing a low-data mode can help reduce the strain on bandwidth, making the AR experience more accessible without sacrificing too much quality.

Example:

L'Oreal faced challenges with providing AR beauty try-ons for users with limited or unstable internet connections. To overcome this, L'Oreal developed a **low-data mode** that allowed users to try on makeup virtually using lower-resolution models, ensuring the app worked seamlessly even in areas with poor internet connectivity.

5. Ensuring Inclusivity and Accessibility for All Users

Challenge:

While AR can offer incredible shopping experiences, businesses must ensure that these experiences are inclusive and accessible to all users, including those with disabilities. For example, individuals with visual impairments may find it difficult to fully engage with AR, and those with motor impairments may struggle with interaction-based AR features that require precise movements.

Solutions:

- **Designing for Accessibility**: Brands should ensure that AR apps are designed with accessibility features in mind, such as voice commands, adjustable contrast, and text-to-speech capabilities. By considering the needs of users with disabilities, businesses can create a more inclusive experience for a wider audience.

- **Adaptive Controls**: Offering multiple interaction modes for AR—such as voice commands, eye-tracking, or simplified controls—can help users with different abilities engage with the AR experience in a way that works best for them.

Example:

Nike has made strides in ensuring that its AR try-on experiences are accessible to a broader audience, including individuals with disabilities. By implementing voice commands and large, easily readable text on AR interfaces, Nike enables users with visual or motor impairments to engage with the app in a more inclusive way.

Conclusion

Ensuring broad consumer adoption of AR and overcoming technological barriers remains one of the biggest challenges for businesses looking to integrate AR into their e-commerce strategies. Issues such as device compatibility, user education, and internet connectivity must be addressed to make AR experiences accessible to a wide range of consumers. By designing AR solutions that are optimized for different devices, offering clear instructions, and ensuring accessibility features for users with disabilities, businesses can foster broader adoption and create engaging, inclusive, and memorable experiences that resonate with today's tech-savvy shoppers.

As AR technology continues to evolve, it is expected that many of these challenges will be mitigated over time. More consumers will adopt AR experiences as the technology becomes more ubiquitous, devices become more capable, and businesses invest in accessible solutions that cater to a diverse range of users. The future of AR in e-commerce holds exciting possibilities, and overcoming these initial barriers will set the stage for even greater consumer engagement and innovation.

CHAPTER 23

PRIVACY AND DATA CONCERNS IN AR

How AR Impacts User Privacy and Data Security in E-Commerce

As Augmented Reality (AR) technology becomes increasingly integrated into e-commerce, it introduces a new set of privacy and data security challenges. AR applications often require users to share personal data, such as location, facial images, and behavioral data, to deliver personalized and immersive experiences. While this data enhances the user experience, it also raises significant concerns about privacy and security.

For businesses implementing AR, it's crucial to balance the need for rich, interactive experiences with the responsibility of protecting user data. Consumer concerns about how their data is collected, used, and protected are at an all-time high, and breaches of privacy can result in loss of trust, legal consequences, and reputational damage. Therefore, companies must adopt robust data security measures and comply with privacy regulations to safeguard their users and their own business interests.

190

This chapter explores how AR impacts user privacy and data security in e-commerce, as well as the real-world challenges faced by businesses when managing sensitive customer information in AR environments.

1. Data Collection and Usage in AR

Challenge:

AR applications typically collect a wide range of data to function effectively. This includes visual data (such as images of the user or their environment), behavioral data (such as interaction patterns), and location data (for geo-targeted AR experiences). The more personalized and immersive the AR experience, the more data the platform collects.

For example, AR-based shopping apps may require access to the user's camera to scan products, track movement, or create virtual try-on experiences. This raises concerns about how this data is used, stored, and shared, particularly when sensitive personal information like facial images, body measurements, or location data is involved.

Solutions:

- **Transparency and Consent**: Brands must be transparent about the data they collect and how it is used. Clearly stated privacy policies and opt-in consent forms are essential to ensure users are aware of what data they are sharing and have control over it.

- **Data Minimization**: Companies should only collect the data that is necessary to provide the AR experience. For example, instead of storing facial images, an AR app could use temporary, anonymized data during the experience and avoid retaining sensitive personal information.

- **Data Anonymization**: Personal data can be anonymized or pseudonymized to reduce the risks associated with data breaches. This ensures that even if data is compromised, it cannot be traced back to individual users.

Example:

Snapchat, known for its AR filters and lenses, has faced scrutiny over how it collects and uses facial data. To address privacy concerns, Snapchat provides users with clear consent requests when activating lenses that use facial recognition, and it has implemented strict policies around data retention, ensuring that images and videos are not stored longer than necessary.

2. Privacy Risks in AR and E-Commerce

Challenge:

The immersive nature of AR can lead to new privacy risks that traditional e-commerce models do not face. Since AR often involves real-time interaction with users' environments, it can capture more sensitive data than typical online shopping platforms. For instance, AR apps might use the camera to scan a user's living room or personal space to visualize how a piece of furniture will look. This raises concerns about how this visual data is handled and whether it could be used inappropriately or exposed to unauthorized parties.

Additionally, AR technology that integrates with social media platforms can lead to an even higher risk of data sharing, as images, interactions, and product preferences are often shared publicly, either intentionally or unintentionally.

Solutions:

- **Strict Access Controls**: AR applications should limit the data they access to what is absolutely necessary. For instance, an AR shopping app that requires the camera for a virtual try-on experience should not have access to the user's location or microphone unless required for the service.

193

- **Clear User Notifications**: Users should be notified when the app is accessing sensitive data, such as their camera or location, and be given the option to decline or modify the permissions granted.

Example:

Google Lens, which is used for AR-powered search and shopping experiences, has been cautious in limiting data collection to only what is needed for the feature. It notifies users about the data being captured and allows them to control the access granted to the app.

---

3. GDPR Compliance and Legal Considerations

Challenge:

The General Data Protection Regulation (GDPR), which governs data protection and privacy in the European Union, is one of the most comprehensive privacy regulations in the world. AR applications in e-commerce that collect personal data must comply with GDPR, which places strict guidelines on how companies collect, store, and process consumer data.

Under GDPR, businesses are required to obtain explicit consent from users before collecting personal data, provide users with the ability to access and delete their data, and ensure that data is protected from unauthorized access. Non-compliance with GDPR can result in heavy fines, reputational damage, and loss of consumer trust.

Solutions:

- **Obtaining Explicit Consent**: Before collecting any personal data through AR, businesses must obtain clear, unambiguous consent from users. This includes providing users with information about the data being collected, its purpose, and how it will be used.
- **Data Access and Deletion**: Companies must provide users with the ability to easily access their personal data, as well as the option to delete it upon request. This can be facilitated through user dashboards or within the app settings.
- **Data Security**: Businesses must implement robust data protection measures, including encryption, secure storage, and regular audits, to ensure that user data is safe from breaches.

Example:

IKEA's AR Place app, which allows users to visualize furniture in their homes, is compliant with GDPR. The app clearly requests permission to access the user's camera and other data, and it does not store any sensitive data without user consent. IKEA has implemented strong security measures to ensure that personal data is protected throughout the customer journey.

4. Data Sharing with Third Parties

Challenge:

Many AR applications in e-commerce require partnerships with third-party service providers for features such as advertising, product recommendations, or cloud storage. However, sharing user data with third parties can introduce additional risks and raise privacy concerns, particularly when users are not fully aware of how their data is being shared.

Solutions:

- **Third-Party Transparency**: Businesses must disclose any third-party data-sharing arrangements in their privacy policies and obtain user consent if their data is shared with external partners. Customers should be made aware of which third parties will have access to their data and how it will be used.
- **Data Processing Agreements**: When sharing data with third parties, businesses should establish data processing agreements that define how the data will be handled, ensuring that third-party partners comply with data privacy laws and standards.
- **Secure Data Transfers**: Companies should use secure methods to transfer data to third-party providers, such as

encryption or anonymization, to mitigate the risks associated with data sharing.

Example:

Facebook's AR Ads feature, which allows advertisers to create AR ads for brands, requires transparency about how consumer data is used for targeted advertising. Facebook's privacy policy outlines how data is collected from users and shared with advertisers, and users are given the option to control their data-sharing preferences.

5. User Trust and Education

Challenge:

Despite the clear benefits AR brings to e-commerce, consumer concerns about privacy and data security remain a significant hurdle to widespread adoption. Users need to feel confident that their personal information is safe and that they are in control of their data. Brands that fail to build trust with users can see increased resistance to adopting AR-powered features.

Solutions:

- **Privacy by Design**: Incorporating privacy as a core principle when designing AR experiences can help build user trust. This includes minimizing data collection, offering clear privacy policies, and ensuring that data is handled securely.

- **Consumer Education**: Educating users on how their data is used and the steps the brand is taking to protect it can go a long way in alleviating privacy concerns. Brands should provide easily accessible information about data usage and privacy controls within their AR apps or websites.

- **Building Trust with Transparency**: Ensuring that consumers are fully informed about their rights and the brand's data practices is key to building long-term trust. Offering transparent data usage policies and easy-to-use privacy settings will encourage users to engage with AR features more freely.

Example:

Apple has established itself as a leader in privacy and data security. Its AR experiences, including those in **Apple ARKit**, are built with privacy considerations in mind. The company provides clear privacy policies and data protection features, educating users about the data collected and empowering them to control their settings.

Conclusion

AR technology in e-commerce offers significant advantages in terms of customer engagement, personalization, and enhanced shopping experiences. However, with the increased use of AR comes the responsibility to protect user privacy and ensure data security. Businesses must navigate the challenges of data collection, third-party sharing, compliance with privacy regulations, and building user trust. By prioritizing transparency, adhering to privacy laws like GDPR, and designing AR experiences with privacy in mind, businesses can harness the power of AR while safeguarding consumer data and maintaining long-term trust.

As AR continues to evolve, addressing privacy and data concerns will be crucial to ensuring its sustainable growth in the e-commerce sector. By striking the right balance between immersive experiences and data protection, brands can build stronger relationships with customers and secure a competitive edge in the marketplace.

CHAPTER 24

EMERGING TRENDS IN AR TECHNOLOGY

The Future of AR Technology and Its Role in Retail

Augmented Reality (AR) has already begun reshaping the landscape of e-commerce, offering immersive and interactive shopping experiences. But as the technology continues to evolve, the potential applications for AR in retail are expanding, and the future of AR in e-commerce looks even more exciting and transformative.

In this chapter, we will explore the emerging trends in AR technology, focusing on the ways AR will continue to enhance retail experiences. These trends include the integration of **AI and machine learning with AR**, the development of **smart glasses** for seamless AR interactions, and the rise of **haptic feedback** and **multi-sensory experiences**. By examining these emerging trends, businesses can better understand how AR will shape the future of retail, allowing them to stay ahead of the curve and capitalize on new opportunities.

1. AI and Machine Learning Integration with AR

Trend   **Overview**:
Artificial Intelligence (AI) and machine learning (ML) are rapidly advancing fields that are being integrated with AR to create more intelligent, adaptive, and personalized shopping experiences. The combination of AI and AR opens up a world of possibilities for e-commerce, making AR experiences smarter, more accurate, and more engaging for users.

- **Personalized AR Shopping**: AI-powered AR applications will enable more personalized shopping experiences, tailoring product recommendations based on past purchases, browsing behavior, and preferences. For example, AR can suggest the perfect size, color, or style of an item by analyzing the user's body shape, face features, or even their mood.

- **Visual Recognition and Search**: Machine learning algorithms can be used to enhance AR's ability to recognize products or objects in the real world, enabling customers to search for similar products in an e-commerce store. For instance, AI could allow users to scan an object in their environment with their phone's camera, and the AR app could suggest matching products or items that are available for purchase.

- **Improved Product Visualization**: AI can optimize the rendering of products in AR, improving the realism and accuracy of product visualizations. For example, AI could help AR apps simulate how a piece of furniture would look under different lighting conditions, in varying environments, or when paired with other products.

Example:

Amazon's **StyleSnap** tool uses AI and machine learning to help users discover fashion items by analyzing a picture. If a customer uploads a photo of an outfit they like, the tool suggests similar products available on Amazon. In the future, AI and AR could combine to show how those items would look on the user in real-time, providing a more personalized shopping experience.

2. Smart Glasses and Wearables for AR Shopping

Trend **Overview**:

The development of **smart glasses** and wearables is one of the most exciting emerging trends in AR technology. While smartphones and tablets have been the primary devices for accessing AR, the future of AR in e-commerce may lie in hands-free, wearable technology that seamlessly integrates AR into daily life.

- **AR Glasses for Immersive Shopping**: Companies like **Microsoft**, **Apple**, and **Google** are investing heavily in smart glasses and wearables that support AR. These devices have the potential to provide a fully immersive AR shopping experience, allowing users to see virtual products overlaid onto their real-world environments without needing to hold a smartphone.

- **In-Store AR Shopping**: Smart glasses could be used in physical stores to guide customers to specific products or display additional product information as they walk through the aisles. For example, a customer could walk into a store, and their AR glasses could automatically highlight sales, promotions, or product details in real-time, enhancing the shopping experience.

- **Hands-Free AR Interaction**: Unlike smartphones, which require users to hold and manipulate the device, smart glasses and wearables allow for hands-free interaction with AR content. This provides more seamless and intuitive interactions, as users can see virtual elements without needing to look down at a screen or use their hands.

Example:

Google's AR Glasses (currently in development) are designed to overlay digital information directly onto the user's field of vision. These glasses could eventually be used for shopping experiences, where a user could walk into a store, view available products through their smart glasses, and access detailed information about those products in real-time.

3. Haptic Feedback and Multi-Sensory AR Experiences

Trend   **Overview**:

As AR technology advances, there is a growing interest in creating multi-sensory AR experiences that go beyond sight and sound. One of the key innovations in this area is **haptic feedback**, which simulates the sense of touch, and it is expected to play a significant role in the future of AR shopping.

- **Haptic Feedback in AR**: Haptic feedback technology can be integrated into AR wearables or smartphones to allow users to feel virtual objects. For example, when using an AR app to try on a piece of clothing or hold a virtual item, haptic feedback would simulate the texture, weight, or shape of the object, adding a physical layer to the virtual experience.

- **Sensory Integration**: In addition to sight and touch, the future of AR may involve integrating other senses, such as smell or taste, into the shopping experience. Imagine a customer experiencing the smell of a perfume or the taste of a virtual food product through an AR-powered interface, providing a deeper, more engaging level of interaction.

- **Enhanced Product Interactions**: Haptic feedback can also be used to simulate interactions with products in a more realistic manner. For instance, if a user is assembling furniture using AR, they could feel the resistance when joining parts, simulating a real-world experience and making the virtual interaction more engaging and tactile.

Example:

Sony has developed **haptic feedback technology** that could be incorporated into AR wearables to provide users with tactile sensations when interacting with virtual products. This technology could allow users to "feel" a virtual pair of shoes or feel the texture of a fabric during a virtual try-on experience, further enhancing the shopping experience.

---

4. AR for Virtual and Social Shopping

Trend   **Overview**:

The future of AR will also be heavily influenced by social commerce and virtual shopping experiences. Consumers increasingly want to shop not just for products, but to engage with friends and influencers during their shopping experience. AR is positioned to bridge the gap between e-commerce and social interaction.

205

- **Virtual Shopping with Friends**: With the integration of AR and social media platforms, users could participate in virtual shopping sessions with their friends. They could try on products together in real-time, share virtual shopping carts, or engage in interactive shopping experiences via AR. This allows for more social and collaborative shopping, which is particularly appealing to younger consumers.

- **Influencer-Driven AR Shopping**: AR will play a key role in influencer-driven e-commerce. As influencers showcase products through AR, their followers will be able to engage directly with the products in a more immersive way, potentially driving higher engagement and sales. Imagine watching an influencer try on clothes virtually, then being able to immediately try the same clothes on in your own home via AR.

- **Live AR Shopping Events**: Future AR shopping platforms may feature live-streamed events where brands and retailers showcase products in an interactive, AR-driven format. Consumers could engage with the products in real-time, participate in virtual try-ons, and purchase items instantly during the live broadcast.

Example:

Instagram has already integrated AR into its shopping features, allowing users to try on makeup products, sunglasses, and more. The future could see an expansion of this, where users can shop together in virtual, shared spaces with their friends or participate in live AR shopping events hosted by brands or influencers.

5. Integration of AR with Blockchain and NFTs

Trend   **Overview**:

One of the more futuristic applications of AR in e-commerce lies in its integration with **blockchain technology** and **Non-Fungible Tokens (NFTs)**. This could revolutionize how digital goods are sold and how customers interact with exclusive or limited-edition products.

- **AR for NFT Shopping**: In the world of digital art and collectibles, AR could be used to display and interact with NFTs in a way that makes them more tangible. Consumers could use AR to view and interact with digital art or collectibles in their homes, blending the virtual and physical worlds.

- **Blockchain Integration for Product Provenance**: For physical products, AR could integrate with blockchain technology to provide real-time proof of authenticity and ownership. This could be particularly useful in industries like luxury goods, where consumers could scan an item using AR to confirm its origin and authenticity via the blockchain.

Example:

Decentraland, a virtual reality platform powered by blockchain, is exploring how AR can be integrated with NFTs, allowing users to view their digital assets in real-world environments through AR. Users could virtually display their NFTs in their living rooms or view them from different angles using AR devices, making digital art feel more real and tangible.

Conclusion

The future of AR in e-commerce is full of exciting potential, with emerging trends like AI integration, smart glasses, haptic feedback, social shopping, and blockchain-driven digital goods paving the way for even more immersive, personalized, and seamless shopping experiences. As AR technology continues to evolve, retailers and businesses must stay ahead of these trends, adopting new technologies and innovative solutions that enhance the shopping experience, improve customer engagement, and drive sales.

By leveraging these emerging trends, businesses can create AR experiences that go beyond traditional online shopping, offering customers a truly transformative way to interact with products, explore new possibilities, and engage with brands in a more meaningful way. The future of AR in retail is bright, and those who embrace these innovations will be well-positioned to lead in the next phase of e-commerce.

CHAPTER 25

THE IMPACT OF AR ON THE RETAIL SUPPLY CHAIN

How AR Will Affect Logistics, Inventory Management, and Supply Chain in E-Commerce

Augmented Reality (AR) is not only transforming the customer-facing aspects of e-commerce, but it is also having a profound impact on the behind-the-scenes operations that drive the retail supply chain. From warehouse management to real-time product tracking, AR is enhancing efficiency, accuracy, and visibility across various stages of the supply chain. By integrating AR technology into logistics and inventory management systems, businesses can improve operational performance, reduce errors, and create more agile supply chains that respond more effectively to customer demand.

This chapter explores how AR is shaping the future of logistics, inventory management, and the overall supply chain in e-commerce. We will look at the various applications of AR in supply chain operations and how businesses are leveraging this technology to streamline processes, enhance worker productivity, and ensure faster, more accurate deliveries.

210

1. AR in Warehouse Management

Challenge:

Warehouses are the backbone of any retail supply chain, and managing inventory, picking, packing, and shipping products efficiently is critical to maintaining a competitive edge. However, traditional warehouse processes can be error-prone and time-consuming, particularly when handling large amounts of inventory. Warehouse workers often rely on paper lists, scanners, and manual checks, all of which can lead to inefficiencies, mistakes, and delays.

How   **AR**   **Helps**:

AR can dramatically improve warehouse operations by providing real-time, visual instructions to workers. By using AR glasses, smartphones, or tablets, warehouse employees can see digital overlays that guide them to the correct location of items, track inventory levels, and even assist with picking and packing.

- **Pick-and-Pack Optimization**: AR can guide workers to the correct locations for order fulfillment, providing step-by-step directions through the warehouse. By overlaying product locations directly onto the worker's view, AR reduces the time spent searching for items and increases accuracy.

- **Real-Time Inventory Tracking**: AR can be used to scan products, track inventory levels, and update stock in real-time. This improves inventory management accuracy and reduces the need for manual stock-taking.

- **Training and Maintenance**: AR can assist with worker training, providing interactive, on-the-job tutorials to improve efficiency and accuracy. Additionally, AR can be used for maintenance, helping workers identify and repair warehouse equipment quickly and effectively.

Example:

DHL, a global logistics company, has implemented AR technology in its warehouses to improve picking accuracy and reduce operational errors. Using smart glasses, warehouse employees receive real-time guidance on the fastest route to pick items, increasing efficiency and reducing picking errors. The system also displays additional product information and instructions, enhancing the workflow and productivity.

2. AR for Real-Time Product Tracking

Challenge:

One of the key challenges in the retail supply chain is tracking products in real-time as they move from suppliers to warehouses and then to customers. Traditional tracking methods, such as

212

barcode scanning, can be slow and prone to errors, especially when handling large volumes of products. Real-time visibility of products in transit is essential for efficient order fulfillment and improving customer satisfaction.

How **AR** **Helps**: AR can provide a more interactive, real-time view of product tracking, offering businesses and consumers alike a detailed and visual understanding of a product's location at any given time. By integrating AR with real-time tracking data from GPS, RFID tags, or IoT devices, businesses can gain greater visibility into their supply chain, track shipments, and even show customers the exact status of their orders.

- **Enhanced Product Tracking**: AR can overlay real-time tracking information onto the user's view of the product or shipment. Warehouse workers, for instance, can scan a product and immediately see its location in the supply chain, including details about its journey, expected arrival time, and current condition.

- **Customer Transparency**: For consumers, AR can provide real-time updates on their order's status, such as delivery times, shipping routes, and estimated arrival. This level of transparency helps improve the customer experience and build trust.

- **Error Prevention and Fraud Detection**: By visualizing tracking data in real-time, businesses can quickly spot discrepancies or issues, reducing the risk of lost, delayed, or misplaced goods. AR can also be used to verify the authenticity of products, preventing fraud.

Example:

FedEx has integrated AR into its logistics operations to provide customers with real-time tracking and visibility. Through an AR app, users can view the current status and location of their packages, overlaying virtual data onto the physical world, which helps to provide a more engaging and informative tracking experience.

3. AR for Inventory Management

Challenge:

Effective inventory management is crucial for e-commerce businesses, as it directly impacts order fulfillment, delivery times, and customer satisfaction. Keeping track of inventory levels in real-time, updating product availability, and forecasting demand are all tasks that require constant attention. Traditional methods of inventory management are often labor-intensive and error-prone, leading to stockouts, overstocking, and inefficient warehouse operations.

How   **AR**   **Helps**:

AR can automate and streamline many aspects of inventory management, offering real-time visibility and enhanced accuracy. By using AR-enabled devices, such as smart glasses or tablets, inventory workers can instantly scan, count, and update stock levels without the need for manual entries or barcode scanning.

- **Real-Time Stock Monitoring**: AR-enabled devices can instantly display up-to-date inventory levels, ensuring workers know exactly how many units are available in real-time. This eliminates the need for manual stock-taking and improves inventory forecasting accuracy.

- **Automated Stock Replenishment**: With AR, inventory management can be automated by providing alerts when stock levels fall below a certain threshold, prompting automatic replenishment orders. This reduces the likelihood of stockouts or overstocking.

- **Efficient Stock Retrieval**: AR can guide warehouse employees to the most efficient locations to retrieve or restock products, saving time and reducing errors. This can be particularly useful in large warehouses with complex layouts.

Example:

Walmart has been using AR to help manage inventory in its warehouses and stores. Using AR, employees are able to quickly find stock locations, check inventory levels, and receive instructions for restocking shelves. This has improved overall inventory accuracy and reduced the time spent searching for products.

---

4. AR for Supply Chain Transparency

Challenge:

Transparency across the supply chain is a major concern for consumers, particularly when it comes to knowing where products come from, how they are manufactured, and the environmental or ethical standards adhered to. As more consumers demand visibility into the supply chains of the products they purchase, businesses must find ways to provide greater transparency and build trust.

How   AR   Helps:

AR can provide an innovative way to showcase product journeys by overlaying information about the product's lifecycle, from manufacturing to distribution. By integrating AR with blockchain or other technologies, businesses can provide consumers with verified, transparent details about a product's history, ensuring authenticity and building customer confidence.

- **Product Storytelling**: With AR, consumers can view the entire history of a product by scanning a QR code or label.

This may include details about the sourcing of raw materials, production processes, and even information about the people involved in making the product.

- **Eco-Friendly and Ethical Supply Chains**: AR can also be used to show how environmentally friendly or ethically sourced products are, helping businesses appeal to conscious consumers who prioritize sustainability.

Example:

Patagonia, known for its commitment to sustainability, uses AR to allow consumers to trace the journey of their products, from sourcing raw materials to the final sale. This transparency helps consumers make informed choices about their purchases, knowing that the product aligns with their ethical values.

5. AR for Enhancing Worker Productivity

Challenge:

E-commerce fulfillment centers and warehouses are often fast-paced environments with high demands for worker productivity and efficiency. Workers must perform tasks quickly while maintaining accuracy to meet customer expectations. However, manual processes and reliance on paper-based instructions can hinder productivity and increase the risk of errors.

How   **AR**   **Helps**:

By providing workers with real-time, hands-free instructions through AR glasses or other wearable devices, businesses can boost worker productivity and reduce errors. AR can also assist with training new employees, enabling them to learn faster and more effectively.

- **Hands-Free Operation**: AR-enabled devices allow workers to view instructions, inventory data, or product details without needing to stop and consult a device or paper document, improving efficiency and accuracy.
- **Training and Onboarding**: AR can be used to create interactive training modules that teach workers how to navigate complex warehouse environments, use machinery safely, or follow specific procedures.

Example:

BMW utilizes AR glasses for assembly line workers. These glasses display step-by-step instructions for assembling car parts, reducing the time spent searching for instructions or consulting manuals. This has improved both worker efficiency and accuracy on the production line.

Conclusion

AR is set to revolutionize the retail supply chain by improving efficiency, accuracy, and transparency at every stage of the process, from warehouse management to product tracking and inventory management. By implementing AR in logistics and supply chain operations, businesses can reduce operational costs, minimize errors, and provide a more seamless experience for customers.

Real-world examples like **DHL**, **IKEA**, **Walmart**, and **Patagonia** demonstrate the transformative potential of AR in supply chain management. As the technology continues to evolve, we can expect further innovations in AR that will enhance operational efficiency, enable real-time tracking, and provide consumers with greater visibility and control over their purchases.

For businesses looking to stay competitive in the e-commerce market, investing in AR technology for supply chain management is not just a trend—it's an essential step toward streamlining operations, reducing costs, and offering a better customer experience.

CHAPTER 26

THE INTEGRATION OF AR AND VIRTUAL REALITY (VR)

How AR and VR Are Converging in E-Commerce

The boundaries between Augmented Reality (AR) and Virtual Reality (VR) are becoming increasingly blurred, particularly in the world of e-commerce. Both AR and VR are immersive technologies that enhance the shopping experience, but they do so in different ways. While AR overlays digital elements onto the real world, VR creates entirely virtual environments that can simulate a new reality.

However, in recent years, there has been a significant convergence of AR and VR technologies, where businesses are integrating both into their e-commerce strategies to create more engaging and immersive shopping experiences. This hybrid of AR and VR is revolutionizing how consumers interact with products, explore virtual stores, and make purchasing decisions.

In this chapter, we will explore how the integration of AR and VR is transforming e-commerce, the benefits of combining these two technologies, and how businesses are leveraging them to enhance the customer experience.

---

1. The Convergence of AR and VR in E-Commerce

Challenge:
AR and VR each serve distinct roles in e-commerce. AR enhances the real world by overlaying digital elements (like product information or virtual try-ons), while VR transports users into entirely digital spaces (like virtual showrooms). The challenge for businesses is to find a way to seamlessly integrate both AR and VR to create a more unified and comprehensive shopping experience.

How   AR   and   VR   Converge:
The convergence of AR and VR in e-commerce allows for richer and more immersive experiences, offering the best of both worlds. This hybrid approach combines AR's ability to superimpose virtual elements on the real world with VR's ability to fully immerse users in a virtual environment. The integration of AR and VR creates opportunities for:

- **Virtual Try-Ons with Real-World Context**: AR can be used for virtual try-ons, allowing users to see how a product looks in their space or on their body, while VR can take that experience a step further by placing users into a fully virtual environment where they can interact with the product in different scenarios or settings.

- **Seamless Shopping Experiences**: Consumers could move seamlessly from interacting with products in AR (such as trying on clothes) to entering a fully immersive VR showroom, where they can explore different product options, attend virtual fashion shows, or experience products in a 360-degree, virtual shopping environment.

- **Hybrid Shopping Environments**: The integration of AR and VR can create hybrid shopping environments where users can both virtually try on clothes (AR) and walk through a fully immersive virtual store (VR). This dynamic combination provides an exciting new way for consumers to interact with products without leaving their homes.

Example:

The North Face, an outdoor apparel retailer, uses both AR and VR in its shopping experiences. The brand created a **VR expedition experience**, where users can virtually explore some of the world's most iconic hiking and climbing destinations. At the same time, they offer AR features, such as a "try-on" feature on their app, allowing consumers to see how outdoor gear might look in their own environment before purchasing. By combining these two technologies, The North Face creates a truly immersive and personalized experience for its customers.

2. VR Showrooms and the Future of Virtual Stores

Trend   **Overview**:
Virtual showrooms powered by VR are a growing trend in e-commerce. Unlike traditional websites or even AR-powered stores, VR showrooms create a fully immersive, 3D environment where users can explore and interact with products just as they would in a physical store. VR showrooms provide a more engaging way for consumers to browse, discover, and interact with products in a virtual space.

- **Fully Immersive Shopping Experiences**: In a VR showroom, users can walk through a virtual store, look at products on virtual shelves, pick them up, rotate them, and even test them out in virtual environments. This experience mimics the tactile and interactive aspects of in-store shopping, which traditional e-commerce sites cannot provide.

- **Product Customization**: VR showrooms allow consumers to interact with products in a fully customizable virtual environment. For example, a customer looking for a new car could explore different models in a VR showroom, customize features, and even simulate a test drive—all from the comfort of their home.

223

- **Enhanced Decision-Making**: By offering immersive, hands-on experiences, VR showrooms allow consumers to make more informed decisions, reducing the likelihood of returns. This is especially valuable for high-ticket items like furniture, electronics, or automobiles, where customers benefit from a more detailed and interactive look at the product before purchasing.

Example:

Audi has implemented a VR showroom where customers can explore and customize cars in 3D before making a purchase. Audi's VR experience allows users to explore every detail of the car, from the exterior to the interior, and customize features such as color, wheels, and interior finishes in a virtual environment. This immersive experience not only provides a fun and engaging shopping experience but also helps customers make more informed decisions.

3. AR/VR Hybrid Experiences in Shopping

Trend   **Overview**:

The combination of AR and VR creates hybrid shopping experiences that provide the best of both worlds. These hybrid experiences enable consumers to transition seamlessly between the physical and virtual realms, combining the practicality of AR with the immersion of VR. This integration has the potential to redefine how consumers engage with products, retailers, and the entire shopping journey.

- **Virtual Store Walkthroughs with AR Product Previews**: Consumers can enter a VR-powered virtual store and explore various product categories, interact with items, and customize their selections. Once they have selected a product, AR can be used to overlay more detailed information, show additional product options, or allow customers to preview the product in their own home. This seamless transition from VR to AR creates a comprehensive shopping experience.

- **Blended Shopping Experiences**: In the near future, consumers may start in a VR showroom to explore a wide range of products and then use AR to try on those products virtually in their own space, providing a more personalized and engaging experience. For example, after virtually testing furniture in a VR living room, a customer could use AR to see how the same furniture would look in their actual living room.

- **Social AR/VR Shopping**: The integration of AR and VR can also facilitate social shopping experiences. Consumers can shop together in a virtual store, interact with products in real-time, and share their AR try-on experiences with friends or family. This creates a more collaborative and social shopping journey, which is

225

particularly appealing to younger generations who value social interactions during their shopping experiences.

Example:

L'Oreal has developed an **AR/VR hybrid experience** where users can attend virtual makeup tutorials or fashion shows (via VR) and then instantly try on makeup products virtually (via AR) to see how the products would look on their face. This hybrid experience combines the excitement and immersion of VR with the practicality of AR, enabling consumers to interact with beauty products in a dynamic and personalized way.

---

4. The Role of AI and Real-Time Data in AR/VR Integration

Trend **Overview**:

The convergence of AR and VR is further enhanced by the integration of **AI** and **real-time data**. AI-powered AR/VR applications are able to respond to user behavior in real-time, offering dynamic, personalized experiences based on the user's preferences, past interactions, and even emotional reactions.

- **Personalized Shopping Journeys**: AI can be used to track a user's interactions within a VR showroom or AR try-on session, adjusting product recommendations, offers, and promotions based on their behavior. For example, if a user spends a long time inspecting a particular product in a VR showroom, the system might suggest related items or offer a personalized discount to encourage purchase.

- **Real-Time Product Interaction**: AI can enhance the interactivity of AR and VR experiences, allowing users to manipulate products in real-time or receive feedback on their actions. This creates a more intuitive and engaging shopping experience, where the system adapts to the user's preferences and behaviors.

Example:

Nike is using AI-powered AR and VR technologies to personalize the shopping experience. When a customer uses Nike's AR app to try on shoes, the app collects data about the user's preferences and interactions, and AI suggests similar shoes or accessories based on past choices. This AI-powered AR experience ensures that users see products tailored to their tastes, improving the likelihood of purchase.

5. The Future of AR and VR in E-Commerce

As the technologies behind AR and VR continue to evolve, we can expect even more sophisticated and seamless integration between these two immersive technologies. In the future, the lines between virtual and physical shopping will continue to blur, enabling consumers to enjoy hybrid shopping experiences that feel as natural and engaging as browsing in a physical store.

The integration of AR and VR in e-commerce will lead to:

- **Highly Interactive Product Demos**: Products will be showcased in fully immersive, interactive environments, allowing consumers to experience and test them in ways that go beyond traditional online browsing.
- **Smarter Shopping Assistants**: AI-powered assistants within AR and VR environments will guide users through the shopping process, provide personalized recommendations, and even help them make purchasing decisions.
- **Seamless Omnichannel Shopping**: The transition from physical stores to virtual environments will become more fluid, allowing consumers to move between in-store, AR, and VR experiences with ease, offering a truly omnichannel shopping journey.

Conclusion

The convergence of AR and VR is set to redefine the future of e-commerce by creating hybrid, immersive shopping experiences that blend the best features of both technologies. Through AR and VR integration, consumers will be able to engage with products in new and exciting ways, from virtual showrooms to personalized try-ons, all while experiencing seamless transitions between the virtual and real world. As businesses adopt these technologies and continue to innovate, the e-commerce landscape will become even more interactive, personalized, and engaging, opening up new opportunities for brands to connect with customers and drive sales in the digital age.

CHAPTER 27

PREPARING FOR THE FUTURE: AR STRATEGIES FOR E-COMMERCE BUSINESSES

Practical Advice for Businesses to Integrate AR into Their Strategies

As AR technology continues to grow in prominence, businesses are increasingly recognizing its potential to transform e-commerce. From enhancing the customer shopping experience to improving supply chain operations, AR offers numerous benefits for e-commerce businesses. However, integrating AR into an e-commerce strategy requires careful planning, the right technological investment, and a clear understanding of how it aligns with business goals.

In this chapter, we will discuss practical advice for businesses looking to integrate AR into their e-commerce strategies. We'll explore the key steps involved in launching AR projects, provide tips for overcoming challenges, and share insights from industry leaders who have successfully implemented AR into their retail strategies.

230

1. Assessing the Need for AR in Your Business

Step 1: Understand Your Objectives
Before diving into AR, businesses should first assess their objectives. What specific problems are you trying to solve with AR? Are you looking to improve product visualization, increase engagement, reduce return rates, or enhance the customer shopping experience? Understanding the purpose of AR integration is critical for ensuring the technology aligns with your business goals.

- **Product Visualization**: If your business deals with products that require detailed inspection, such as furniture, fashion, or cosmetics, AR can help customers better visualize how products will fit into their environment or how they will look on them.
- **Customer Engagement**: AR offers interactive and immersive experiences that can keep customers engaged. Think about offering fun, gamified experiences or personalized shopping journeys that encourage customers to explore and interact with your products.
- **Reducing Return Rates**: If returns are a major issue for your business, AR can help customers make more informed purchasing decisions, thereby reducing the likelihood of returns. By allowing users to virtually try

231

products, they can see how an item fits or looks before purchasing.

Example:

Warby Parker, the eyewear brand, implemented AR to allow customers to virtually try on glasses before making a purchase. This helped them address the challenge of product visualization, reduce returns, and improve customer satisfaction by giving customers a better idea of how the glasses would look on them.

---

2. Choose the Right AR Tools and Platforms

Step 2: Select AR Development Tools
Once you've determined the objectives for your AR project, the next step is to select the appropriate tools and platforms to bring your vision to life. There are a variety of AR development platforms, each with different features, capabilities, and pricing models.

- **ARKit (for iOS)**: If your target audience is primarily iPhone and iPad users, ARKit is a powerful tool for developing AR applications. It allows for features such as motion tracking, environment mapping, and object recognition.

- **ARCore (for Android)**: Similarly, ARCore is Google's development platform for Android devices. ARCore offers similar functionality to ARKit and is designed to help developers create immersive AR experiences for Android users.

- **WebAR**: If you want to offer AR experiences without requiring users to download a dedicated app, WebAR allows for AR integration directly within a browser. This is a great option for businesses that want to provide AR features on their website or through social media platforms.

- **AR Development Agencies**: If your business lacks the in-house technical expertise to build AR applications, consider partnering with an AR development agency. These agencies specialize in creating customized AR experiences and can help bring your vision to life more quickly and efficiently.

Example:

IKEA uses **ARCore** and **ARKit** to develop their popular **IKEA Place** app, allowing users to visualize furniture in their own homes using their smartphones. This app is built on both of these platforms to provide seamless AR experiences for both Android and iOS users.

3. Start Small and Scale Gradually

Step 3: Start with a Pilot Project
When implementing AR into your e-commerce strategy, it's often wise to start small. Begin with a pilot project that focuses on one specific area of your business, such as a single product line or a specific feature like virtual try-ons or product visualization. This allows you to test the waters, measure the effectiveness of the technology, and understand what works before expanding to a larger scale.

- **Test with a Specific Audience**: Select a small group of customers or users to test the AR experience. Gather feedback on their experiences to identify pain points, areas for improvement, and any technical issues that need to be addressed.
- **Refine the Experience**: Use the data and feedback from the pilot project to refine the AR experience. Optimize the technology, user interface, and content to ensure that the final product is engaging, functional, and user-friendly.

Example:
Sephora took a gradual approach when introducing AR with its **Virtual Artist** feature. The initial rollout allowed customers to virtually try on makeup through a mobile app. Based on user feedback, Sephora iterated on the design, expanding the selection

of makeup products and refining the user experience before launching the feature to a broader audience.

4. Integrating AR into the Customer Journey

Step 4: Seamlessly Integrate AR into the Shopping Experience
For AR to truly enhance your e-commerce strategy, it must be integrated into the broader customer journey. Think about how AR can complement and enhance existing touchpoints within the shopping process, such as product discovery, purchasing, and post-purchase engagement.

- **Product Discovery**: Use AR to allow customers to visualize products in their environment before making a purchase. For example, furniture retailers like **Wayfair** use AR to let customers see how a sofa or table will look in their living room.

- **Virtual Try-Ons**: Incorporating AR into fashion, beauty, and accessories allows customers to virtually try on products before committing to a purchase. This is particularly effective in reducing return rates and increasing customer confidence in their decisions.

- **Checkout and Post-Purchase**: AR can also enhance the post-purchase experience by providing additional content or tutorials related to the purchased product. For instance, after buying a product, customers could use AR to receive setup instructions or maintenance tips.

Example:

L'Oreal's **AR Try-On** experience lets users try on makeup virtually before buying. After purchasing, L'Oreal integrates post-purchase AR experiences, such as makeup tutorials or styling tips, helping to enhance the overall customer journey and increase engagement with the brand.

5. Measure Success and Optimize

Step 5: Monitor Performance and Optimize
As with any technological implementation, it's important to track the performance of your AR strategy and optimize it over time. Use data analytics to measure customer engagement, sales, return rates, and other key performance indicators (KPIs). This will help you understand the impact of AR on your business and identify areas for improvement.

- **Track User Engagement**: Monitor how often customers interact with your AR features and how long they engage with them. High engagement rates typically indicate that users find value in the AR experience.

- **Conversion Rates and ROI**: Analyze how AR influences purchase decisions by tracking conversion rates before and after AR integration. Are customers more likely to buy after interacting with a virtual try-on or visualizing a product in their environment?
- **Feedback Loops**: Continuously collect feedback from customers to identify pain points and areas for improvement. Regularly update your AR experiences based on this feedback to keep them fresh and engaging.

Example:

Nike uses AR technology to allow users to try on shoes virtually. After analyzing engagement data, Nike optimized the AR feature by adding more shoe models and refining the interface to increase conversion rates and customer satisfaction.

---

6. Stay Ahead of the Curve: Innovations in AR Technology

Step   6:   Keep   Innovating
The world of AR is rapidly evolving, and what works today may not be as effective tomorrow. It's essential for businesses to stay ahead of the curve by keeping an eye on emerging trends and new technologies.

237

- **AI and Machine Learning Integration**: As AI and machine learning continue to advance, integrating these technologies with AR will allow for even more personalized and dynamic experiences. For example, AR could recommend products based on a customer's facial expression, behavior, or preferences.

- **AR Glasses and Wearables**: As smart glasses and wearables become more mainstream, they will provide opportunities for businesses to offer even more immersive and hands-free AR experiences. Prepare for the future by researching AR wearables and how they might fit into your business strategy.

Example:

Gucci has started using AR to create virtual try-on experiences for its luxury products. As smart glasses and wearables evolve, Gucci could expand its use of AR to create an even more immersive, real-time shopping experience, allowing customers to try on and explore products without needing to use their smartphones.

Conclusion

Integrating AR into your e-commerce strategy can significantly enhance the customer experience, increase engagement, and boost sales. However, successful implementation requires careful planning, the right technology, and a thoughtful approach to integrating AR into the customer journey. By starting small, tracking performance, and optimizing based on feedback, businesses can harness the full potential of AR to create immersive, personalized, and engaging shopping experiences.

The future of AR in e-commerce is full of opportunities, and those who embrace it now will be well-positioned to lead in an increasingly digital, immersive retail landscape. Through continuous innovation and strategic planning, AR will continue to reshape the way we shop and interact with products, creating new possibilities for businesses and consumers alike.

www.ingramcontent.com/pod-product-compliance
Lightning Source LLC
LaVergne TN
LVHW051321050326
832903LV00031B/3284

* 9 7 9 8 3 1 5 8 8 4 8 7 3 *